Picture Book Parties!

Picture Book Parties!

Kimberly M. Hutmacher

LIBRARIES UNLIMITED

AN IMPRINT OF ABC-CLIO, LLC
Santa Barbara, California • Denver, Colorado • Oxford, England

Library of Congress Cataloging-in-Publication Data

Hutmacher, Kimberly.
   Picture book parties! / Kimberly M. Hutmacher.
     p. cm.
   Includes bibliographical references and index.
     ISBN 978–1–59884–772–7 (pbk. : acid-free paper) — ISBN 978–1–59884–773–4 (ebook)
1. School libraries—Activity programs—United States. 2. Picture books for children—United States—Bibliography. 3. Activity programs in education—United States. 4. Reading (Elementary)—Activity programs. 5. Family literacy programs—United States. 6. Reading promotion—United States. I. Title.
Z675.S3H88   2011
027.62′51—dc22   2010054448

ISBN: 978–1–59884–772–7
EISBN: 978–1–59884–773–4

15 14 13 12 11   1 2 3 4 5

This book is also available on the World Wide Web as an eBook.
Visit www.abc-clio.com for details.

Libraries Unlimited
An Imprint of ABC-CLIO, LLC

ABC-CLIO, LLC
130 Cremona Drive, P.O. Box 1911
Santa Barbara, California 93116-1911

This book is printed on acid-free paper ∞

Manufactured in the United States of America

Illustrations by Ron Hutmacher. Used with permission.

The author would like to dedicate this book to her family for providing endless inspiration, love, and support.

Contents

Acknowledgments

Our very special thanks to Ronald A. Hutmacher for designing and illustrating all of the black line template pages.

Introduction

The popularity of family reading nights and special literacy events inspired me to write this book. *Picture Book Parties!* is a resource to help teachers, librarians, and literacy coaches celebrate popular picture books and their creators with students and their families. Each of the first 25 chapters of this book is dedicated to a specific story time theme. For each theme, I recommend four–five picture books to read. The recommended books are paired with games and center activities.

When to Use This Book

1. Use this book to plan the perfect family reading event for your class and/or school.
2. Use this book to plan a fun story time in your classroom or library.

Benefits of Using This Book

1. This book is a time saver. *Picture Book Parties!* contains 25 complete party plans/story times.
2. The activities contain clear concise directions to help busy teachers and librarians navigate easily and quickly.
3. The activities are fun.
4. The activities are inexpensive.
5. The activities are not only fun, simple, and inexpensive; they will also help you meet state education standards.

A Few Tips

1. These celebrations are flexible. These parties can happen during your regular story time, each celebration can be broken up over several days, or you can host special literacy events that welcome students and their families.
2. For those of you that choose to use this book to help plan and organize family nights and/or other literacy events, Appendix A contains a themed party invitation template for each story time. Students can fill in the place, date, and time; color the invitations; and take them home to their families.

3. Appendix B contains templates to help complete some of the games and center activities suggested in this book.

4. Although most of the books, games, and center activities listed are recommended for preschool and early elementary grades (ages four–five), I have also included one–two picture books that older students might enjoy in each group of recommended titles. Those titles are marked with an asterisk (*). I have tried to include one–two activities in each chapter that older students would find appealing as well. Those activities are also marked with an asterisk (*).

5. In "Chapter 26: Readers and Authors, Making a Lasting Connection," I offer many ideas to help bring your students and book creators together. I talk about author studies, in-person visits, virtual visits, funding visits, and so much more.

6. On page 121 you will find a complete picture book bibliography of titles celebrated in this book.

7. I've also included an index to help you quickly find what you are looking for.

How to Use this Book

1. Browse through the book, and choose your theme.
2. Make a copy of the corresponding invitation black line for each student.
3. Have students color the invitations and fill in the place, date, and time. Send invitations home to parents.
4. A few days prior to the event, gather the books and any supplies you will need to complete any of the activities.
5. Make copies of any black line activity sheets you will need.
6. Do any precutting that needs to be done.
7. The day of the big event, organize the centers in your party space.
8. Look over your party plan one last time to be sure you have not forgotten anything.
9. When your guests arrive, welcome them to the party. Feel free to keep your party plan close by to refer to just in case you need it.

My greatest hope is that this book will serve as a guide to help your students make lasting friendships with characters and lasting connections with stories and their creators.

Welcome to the party!

1

Wild Book Ramble

> **Featured Books**
>
> *Where the Wild Things Are* by Maurice Sendak
> *Go Away, Big Green Monster* by Ed Emberley
> *Monster Mama* by Liz Rosenberg
> *The Gruffalo's Child* by Julia Donaldson
> **Jumanji* by Chris Van Allsberg

Party Games

Monster Says

In this game, the leader will be like Mama in *Monster Mama* by Liz Rosenberg. The leader will teach the group how to be good monsters. This game is played just like Simon Says.

- The leader gives a simple instruction to the group. For example, "Monster says, roar like a monster!"
- The group does what the leader says, unless the leader does not say "Monster says . . . " first.
- Other examples of monster things that the leader might ask the group to do would be to jump up and down, make a funny face, and say, "Boo!"

Wild Romp Freeze

In honor of *Where the Wild Things Are* by Maurice Sendak, turn the music up.

- Encourage your guests to make like monsters and dance and dance and dance.
- When the light is switched off though, they must freeze.
- Anyone who keeps dancing once the light is off is out.
- Any little monsters still standing after three rounds, can be crowned kings and queens of the Wild Romp Freeze.
- It might be nice to have toy plastic or homemade construction paper crowns for the winners to wear.

Party Centers

Art: Monster Peek-a-Boo Faces

What you will need: two paper plates for each guest, markers, crayons, colored pencils, paper punch, yarn cut into five-inch pieces.

Before your group arrives:

- Punch one hole in the top of each plate.

When your guests arrive, demonstrate and give the following directions:

- Draw a monster face on the front of one of the plates.
- Encourage creativity with the monsters. They can be any kind of monster the guests would like.
- Write peek-a-boo in the center of the front of the second plate.
- Place the peek-a-boo plate on top of the monster face plate and line up the holes at the top.
- Feed the piece of yarn through the holes and tie it in a bow.
- Now, just like Ed Emberley's *Big Green Monster*, they can see their monster when they want to, and they can make it disappear when they want to.

Writing: If I Were a Monster . . .

What you will need: writing paper and pencils.

- Ask your guests to write three sentences describing what they would look and act like if they were a monster.
- Would they be funny, happy, sad, mean, kind, etc.?
- You might ask older elementary students to write a story about their monster.

Science: Shadow Creatures

Begin this activity by explaining that shadows form when an object or person blocks a light source. Show students the shadows in the book *The Gruffalo's Child* by Julia Donaldson.

What you will need: a sunny day, a bulk roll of white paper cut into sections large enough to trace a body, pencils, markers, crayons, and scissors.

- Take your guests outside into a sunny area.
- Partner guests into groups of two.
- Ask each person to lay out his/her piece of paper. They need to lay their paper so that when they stand next to it, their shadow is formed on the paper.
- Ask one person from each group to take their best monster or wild animal pose, and ask their partner to trace the shadow of the pose onto the paper.
- The partners switch places.
- Color their tracing.
- Cut out the creatures and display them down a long hallway. You could call it your Hall of Monsters.

Technology

*Chris Van Allsberg's Web site has many video clips of himself discussing his books and the process he goes through to write and illustrate them. Older elementary students would probably enjoy these the most. Click here to view the video clips: http://www.chrisvanallsburg.com/videoclips.html.

*Guests of all ages will enjoy the scavenger hunt game on his site. Click here to play it: http://www.chrisvanallsburg.com/scavengerhunt.html.

*Party Snack

Monster Cookies

What you will need: a premade sugar cookie for each guest; vanilla frosting divided into single serving cups; red, brown, and black licorice strings (monster hair) cut into five-inch pieces; chocolate chips, colorful sprinkles and decors, plastic knives, paper plates, and napkins.

Demonstrate and give the following directions:

- Spread the frosting on the cookie.
- Design your very own monster face on your cookie with the decorations provided.

2

Fairy Tale Free-for-All

> **Featured Books**
>
> *The Princess and the Pizza* by Mary Jane Auch
> *Somebody and the Three Blairs* by Marilyn Tolhurst
> *The Stinky Cheese Man and Other Fairly Stupid Tales* by Jon Scieszka
> *The Frog Prince Continued* by Jon Scieszka
> *Once Upon a Cool Motorcycle Dude* by Kevin O'Malley

Party Game

Caught with the Crown

What you will need: a toy crown.
This game is played just like Hot Potato.

- Turn up the music and pass the crown around the circle.
- When the music stops, whoever has the crown in their hands is out.
- Continue to play rounds until the last prince or princess is left standing.
- Award the winner with the crown.

Party Centers

Writing: If I Were a Fairy Tale Character . . .

What you will need: note cards, Template 1 in Appendix B, drawing paper, pencils, markers, and crayons.

Before your guests arrive:

- Write one common fairy tale character on each note card. Some characters you might include are prince, princess, knight, wolf, fox, frog, dragon, pig, giant, and witch.

When your group is ready, give the following directions:

- Choose one character and think about what they would be like if they were that character.

- Answer the questions about their character on the Template 1 worksheet provided in Appendix B.
- Draw a picture of your character on the drawing paper.
- Older students might want to write and illustrate an entire story about their character.

Math: Sizing Up the Three Bears

What you will need: five teddy bears in various sizes, a different colored ribbon to tie around each bear.

The story of *Somebody and the Three Blairs* provides an excellent opportunity to talk about size and ordering by size.

Before your guests arrive:

- Tie a different colored ribbon around each bear.

When your group is ready, give the following directions:

- Line the bears up in order of smallest to largest. When you are finished lining them up, answer the following questions:

Which bear is smallest?

Which bear is largest?

Which bear is in the middle?

Now practice ordinal counting.

Which bear is second in line?

Which bear is fourth in line?

*Art: My Own Royal Shield

What you will need: copies of Template 2 in Appendix B, pieces of cardboard (empty pizza boxes cut in half would be just the right size for this project), pencils, markers.

Begin this activity by reminding guests that we often see knights carrying shields to protect themselves in fairy tales. Take this opportunity to point out the pictures of the characters carrying shields in the book *Once Upon a Cool Motorcycle Dude* by Kevin O'Malley. Explain that in medieval times, shields served as more than just protection for knights. The symbols on the shield told about the knight's family and his life.

When your group is ready, demonstrate and give the following directions:

- Cut out the template shield.
- Use this template to trace the shield onto a piece of cardboard, or if they wish, they can freehand their own symbol.
- Cut out the cardboard shield.

Note: Depending on the grade of cardboard, it can sometimes be difficult to cut. If this is the case with your cardboard, you may want to precut the shields with a box cutter.

The cardboard is meant to make the shields sturdier, but you could always just have them cut out the template and decorate it without using the cardboard.

- Draw symbols on your shields that tell a little bit about your family and life.
- This is a great activity for families to work on together. When everyone is finished, ask families to display their shields and share what their symbols mean.

Technology

*Guests can view animated Hans Christian Andersen Fairy Tales on this Web site: http://andersenfairytales.com/en/main.

*Guests can view animated Grimm's Fairy Tales on this Web site: http://www.grimmfairytales.com/en/main.

*Party Snack

Royal Pizza

In honor of *The Princess and the Pizza* by Mary Jane Auch, you and your guests can make and enjoy this simple and delicious snack.

What you will need: toasted English muffins sliced in half (enough for each guest to have one slice), pizza sauce, shredded mozzarella cheese, pepperoni slices, plastic spoons, paper plates, small cups, and napkins.

Before your guests arrive:

- Divide the sauce, cheese, and pepperoni slices into individual serving cups.

When your group is ready, demonstrate and give the following directions:

- Spoon sauce over English muffin.
- Sprinkle with shredded mozzarella cheese.
- Top with two–three pepperoni slices.
- Microwave on paper plate for 20 seconds or until cheese is melted. Enjoy!

3

All Aboard the Book Train

Before your guests arrive, set your chairs up in two rows of two, just like the inside of a train. You might want to set a small bell on each chair. These can be purchased inexpensively from party stores or dollar stores. Also, encourage your guests to wear their pajamas to this party. They will truly feel like passengers on *The Polar Express* by Chris Van Allsberg.

Trains by Lynn Curlee is a long book and would probably be best enjoyed in its entirety by older elementary students. However, even if you choose not to read this entire book to your group, you might want to begin your party by reading some excerpts from the book on the history of trains. This book also has many wonderful train illustrations.

Party Game

Conductor Catnap

What you will need: a few keys on a key ring, a scarf to blindfold the conductor.

When your group is ready, give the following directions:

- Ask your guests to sit in a circle.
- Invite one of your guests to be the sleepy conductor.
- Blindfold the conductor.
- Place the keys somewhere near the conductor.
- Have one guest quietly grab the keys and sit back down.
- The conductor who took his short catnap can remove his blindfold.
- He gets three opportunities to guess who took his train keys.
- If he guesses correctly, he gets another turn.

- If he does not guess correctly, the person who took the keys gets a turn as conductor.
- The game continues like this until each guest has had a turn as conductor and/or hiding the keys.

Party Centers

Dramatic Play

What you will need: two–three empty large appliance boxes, markers, box cutter
Stores that sell appliances often have empty boxes that they are happy to donate.

Before your guests arrive:

- Using the box cutter, cut out doors and windows into each of your boxes.
- Line the boxes up like train cars.

When your guests arrive:

- Encourage your group to use the markers to decorate the train, and then play inside of it.

Math: Cargo Sort

What you will need: four–five shoe boxes, four–five different kinds of cargo (examples: cotton balls, buttons, beads, paperclips, chalk).

Before your guests arrive:

Line your shoe boxes up like train cars.

When your group is ready, demonstrate and give the following directions:

- Sort the cargo, with each different kind of cargo going into its own train car.
- When they are finished, ask them which car has the most cargo?
- Which car has the least?

*Science: Train Whistles

What you will need: a clean, empty plastic soda bottle for each guest, markers, glitter, glue, stickers.
Begin this activity by explaining the science behind a whistle. Explain that air enters one end of the whistle when we blow into it. The air collects and creates pressure at the other mostly closed end of the whistle. Sound is made when air escapes a teeny tiny hole at this end. Remind guests about the sound of the train whistle in *The Whistle on the Train* by Margaret Mcnamara.

When your group is ready, demonstrate and give the following directions:

- Decorate the outside of their bottles (whistles) any way they wish.
- After the whistles are decorated, blow across the bottle's opening and listen for the train whistle.

- Now explain how different train whistles mean different things. One short whistle means, stop. Two long whistles mean, go. Three short whistles mean, back up. The Midwest Central Railroad has a more complete chart of whistle sounds and their meanings: http://www.mcrr.org/PAGES/kidsWhistle.html.
- Have your guests practice making each kind of whistle sound.

Art: What Kind of Train Car Are You?

We learn all about the different types of train cars in the book *Freight Train* by Donald Crews.

What you will need: rectangular pieces of construction paper, crayons, markers, and colored pencils.

When your group is ready, give the following directions:

- Draw the kind of car you like best and share it with the group. Will it be a hopper car, a caboose, a box car, a gondola car, a cattle car, or a steam engine?

*Technology

The Pennsylvania Department of Transportation has a train Web site for kids. It is full of educational information and also has a fun Lego train game: http://www.dot.state.pa.us/Internet/pdKids.nsf/TrainHomePage?OpenFrameset

Trakkies is a Web site dedicated to kids who love trains. They have games and activities for younger children ages 5–7 and older children ages 8–12: http://www.familyandfriends-railcard.co.uk/cardholders/kidszone

*Party Snack

Fruit Train

This snack is super simple, yummy, and educational.

What you will need: kabob sticks, presliced apples, bananas, strawberries and grapes, paper plates, and napkins.

When your group is ready, demonstrate and give the following directions:

- Slide each slice of fruit onto the kabob.
- Challenge them to create a pattern. Example: one apple slice, two banana slices, two grapes and one strawberry slice.

4

Bear Bonanza

Featured Books

Blueberries for Sal by Robert McCloskey
Corduroy by Don Freeman
We're Going on a Bear Hunt by Michael Rosen
The Teddy Bear's Picnic by Jimmy Kennedy
*Alaska's Three Bears by Shannon Cartwright

Note: Ask each guest to bring their favorite teddy bear. You might want to have extras on hand in case anyone forgets.

Party Game

Teddy Bear Hide and Seek

This game is inspired by the game of hide and seek played in Jimmy Kennedy's book, *The Teddy Bear's Picnic.*

Before your guests arrive:

- Hide a teddy bear somewhere in the room where the party will be held.

When your group is ready:

- One at a time, each guest will have the opportunity to guess where the teddy bear is hidden.
- You will respond with, "You are getting warmer," if they are getting closer to the hiding place.
- You will respond with, "You are getting colder," if they are getting farther away from the hiding place.
- The game continues like this until the teddy bear is found.

Party Centers

Dramatic Play

- Have your guests act out the actions as you read the book, *We're Going on a Bear Hunt* by Michael Rosen.

- For example, they can motion with their arms like they are swimming through the river, take large exaggerated steps like they are wading through mud, etc.

Writing: Bear Facts

What you will need: writing paper, pens, and pencils.

When your group is ready, give the following directions:

- Ask your guests to remember what they learned about bears in the book *Alaska's Three Bears* by Shannon Cartwright.
- Have them write three facts that they remember from the book.
- Older students can be asked to write more.
- When they are finished, each guest can share the facts they remembered with the group.

Math: Button Bonanza

This is a wonderful activity to do after you have read the book *Corduroy* by Don Freeman.

What you will need: a variety of buttons in different colors, small cups to use for sorting, paper, and pencils.

When your group is ready, give the following directions:

- Sort the buttons by color into the individual cups.
- Count how many they have of each color.
- Record the colors and amounts on the paper.

Art: More Button Fun

This activity further celebrates the book *Corduroy* by Don Freeman.

What you will need: one larger button for each guest (large enough that you can use yarn to sew it, rather than thread), a copy of Template 4 from Appendix B, yarn, plastic needles, scissors, crayons, markers.

Before your guests arrive:

- Trace the pocket from Template 4 Appendix B onto a piece of construction paper (for each guest).

When your group is ready, demonstrate and give the following directions:

- Cut out the pocket with the scissors.
- Demonstrate how to thread the needle with the yarn and how to tie off the end.
- Find a place on the pocket where you would like the button to go.
- Demonstrate how to sew the button onto the pocket, feeding the needle in one hole and then feeding it up the second hole.

- Demonstrate how to tie the yarn off on the back.
- Use crayons and markers to further decorate the pockets.

*Technology

National Geographic Kids has photos, videos, fun facts and activities about both brown bears and polar bears.

For brown bears: http://kids.nationalgeographic.com/Animals/CreatureFeature/Brown-bear.

For polar bears: http://kids.nationalgeographic.com/Animals/CreatureFeature/Polar-bear.

*Party Snack

Blueberry Shortcake

This snack is a nice tie-in with the book *Blueberries for Sal* by Robert McCloskey.

What you will need: fresh or frozen blueberries (thawed), shortcakes or slices of pound cake, whipped topping, paper plates, plastic spoons, napkins.

Demonstrate and give the following directions:

- Place the shortcake slice on a paper plate.
- Top with a spoon full of blueberries.
- Top with a spoon full of whipped topping. Yum!

5

A Rainbow of Reading Fun

Featured Books

A Color of His Own by Leo Leonni
Brown Bear, Brown Bear, What Do You See? by Bill Martin Jr.
My Many Colored Days by Dr. Seuss
Harold and the Purple Crayon by Crockett Johnson
*A Color Sampler by Kathleen Westray

Encourage guests to dress in their favorite color for this party.

Party Game

Red Light, Green Light, Blue Light, Orange Light

Get the party started by playing a bit of an altered version of the classic Red Light, Green Light. It is easier to play this game in a large gymnasium or a large open area outside.

What you will need: construction paper in various colors.

When your group is ready:

- Line guests up along one wall of the room as if they were going to race each other.
- Explain what each of the colors you hold up mean. Green light means go. Red light means stop. Yellow means slow down. Options for other colors include: blue means crawl. Orange means hop. Purple means roll. You are free to come up with alternative actions for these colors, too.
- Explain that guests will do the action of whatever color you hold up.
- If someone performs the wrong action, they must go back to the beginning and start again.
- The person who makes it to the other wall or finish line first wins!

Party Centers

*Art: Creating Colors

This activity celebrates the book *A Color Sampler* by Kathleen Westray.

What you will need: tempera paint in red, yellow, blue, black, and white; paper plates; paint brushes.

- Begin by reminding guests that red, yellow, and blue are primary colors. They are the only colors that cannot be made by mixing other colors. Ask guests to create secondary colors by mixing the following color combinations on their plates:
- Red + Yellow = Orange   Yellow + Blue = Green   Blue + Red = Violet
- Encourage older students to go a step farther. Ask them to mix one primary color with one secondary color to make the following intermediate colors:
- Red + Violet = Red-Violet   Red + Orange = Red-Orange   Violet + Blue = Blue-Violet
- Orange + Yellow = Yellow-Orange   Yellow + Green = Yellow-Green   Blue + Green = Blue-Green
- Demonstrate how adding white to a color will lighten the shade and adding black to a color will darken the shade. Ask guests to give it a try!

Writing: What Color Are You?

This writing exercise celebrates *My Many Colored Days* by Dr. Seuss.
What you will need: lined writing paper, pencils and/or pens.

When your group is ready, give the following directions:

- Recall the different colors in this book and how they made the author feel.
- What color do you feel like?
- Write about why you feel like that color.

Math: Animal Sequencing

This activity will help students recall the order of events in the book *Brown Bear, Brown Bear, What Do You See?* by Bill Martin Jr.

What you will need: plastic animals such as a bear, a bird, a duck, a horse, a frog, a cat, a dog, a sheep, and a fish. Plastic animals can often be found in sets at dollar stores or you can trace and cut your own from card stock.

When your group is ready, give the following directions:

- Put the animals in the order in which they appear in the book *Brown Bear, Brown Bear, What Do You See?* by Bill Martin Jr.

Science: Camouflage Creatures

This activity celebrates the book *A Color of His Own* by Leo Lionni.
What you will need: white construction paper, crayons, various colors of cellophane.

Begin by discussing what camouflage is and why animals use it. Explain how it is used to protect them from their enemies. By being able to turn into any color he is on, the chameleon is in a constant state of camouflage.

When your group is ready, demonstrate and give the following directions:

- Draw a chameleon on the white construction paper and color it in.
- Demonstrate how the chameleon can change color each time a different color of cellophane is placed on top of it.
- Encourage guests to experiment with different colors on their chameleons.

Technology

*Mix primary colors with the Mix and Match tool at Exploratorium: http://www.exploratorium.edu/exhibits/mix_n_match/

You will find many coloring pages, crafts, and games and the official Web site of Crayola: http://www.crayola.com/

*Party Snack

Purple Ice Cream Floats

This recipe celebrates the color purple and the book *Harold and the Purple Crayon* by Crockett Johnson.

What you will need: vanilla ice cream, grape soda, cups, spoons, straws, napkins, and ice cream scoop

When your group is ready, demonstrate and give the following directions:

- Place one scoop of vanilla ice cream into the cup.
- Pour grape soda into the cup until it just covers the ice cream.
- Serve with a spoon and a straw. Enjoy!

6

Friend Fest

Featured Books

My Friend Rabbit by Eric Rohman
Don't Need Friends by Carolyn Crimi
The Rainbow Fish by Marcus Pfister
Frog and Toad Are Friends by Arnold Lobel
*Owen and Mzee: The True Story of a Remarkable Friendship
by Isabella Hatkoff, Craig Hatkoff, and Dr. Paula Kahumbu

Party Game

Three-Leg Race

This party game will require true cooperation between friends. This game should be played outside or in a gymnasium.

What you will need: burlap bags and a whistle.

When your group is ready:

- Pair up your guests and line them up at the start line.
- Demonstrate with a volunteer how each pair of friends is supposed to place their inside legs into the bag and how to move together cooperatively to get to the finish line.
- When you are ready, blow the whistle and let the race begin.
- The first pair to the finish line wins.

Party Centers

**Writing: Letter to a Friend*

What you will need: lined writing paper, pens/pencils.

- Remind your guests how Frog wrote a letter to Toad in the book *Frog and Toad Are Friends* by Arnold Lobel.
- Ask your guests to write a letter to one of their friends.

Math: Sizing Up Animal Friends

What you will need: a copy of the book *My Friend Rabbit* by Eric Rohman.

When your group is ready, give the following directions:

- Turn to the page towards the middle of the book that shows all of the animals standing up, one on top of the other.
- Order the animals from largest to smallest.
- Count the animals, practicing ordinal numbers: first, second, third, etc.

Art: Fish Friend

This activity celebrates the book *The Rainbow Fish* by Marcus Pfister.
What you will need: a copy of Template 3 in Appendix B for each guest, small squares of tissue paper in a variety of colors, scissors, and glue.

When your group is ready, demonstrate and give the following directions:

- Cut out the fish from the template. Note: Guests could also choose to draw their own fish.
- Glue the tissue paper squares on the fish.
- Encourage creativity and originality. The fish does not have to look like the fish from the book. Guests can choose their own color combinations and patterns.

*Technology

This Web site celebrates *Owen and Mzee: The True Story of a Remarkable Friendship* written by Isabella Hatkoff, Craig Hatkoff, and Dr. Paula Kahumbu. Visitors to the site can go on a butterfly hunt and participate in a banana leaf race. They can also print coloring pages and Owen and Mzee cutouts. They can view their home in Haller Park and learn more about these good friends and their everyday life. http://www.owenandmzee.com/omweb/activitypages.html

Party Snack

Friendship Sandwiches

Remind guests how the friends shared a sandwich in the book *Don't Need Friends* written by Carolyn Crimi.
What you will need: long loaves of French bread sliced down the middle, peanut butter, jelly, plastic knives, plates, napkins, and a knife to slice the sandwich into individual servings.

When your group is ready, demonstrate and give the following directions:

- With the loaf open faced, spread peanut butter on one side of the loaf and jelly on the other side.
- Close the loaf and cut the sandwich into individual servings. Eat up!

7

Pigeon Party

Pigeons by Miriam Schlein has a lot of text and may be too long to read in its entirety. However, this book is full of interesting facts about pigeons and engaging photographs. I recommend that you show the photos and choose some of the more pertinent pigeon facts to share.

Party Game

Feed a Pigeon

What you will need: a scarf to use as a blindfold, gummy worms, plates.

- Gather your guests in a circle.
- Choose one person to be the pigeon.
- Blindfold the pigeon with the scarf.
- Place a gummy worm on a plate.
- Choose someone to be the worm keeper.
- Have the worm keeper retrieve the plate and hide it behind them.
- Remove the blindfold from the hungry pigeon.
- The hungry pigeon gets three chances to guess who has the worm.
- If he guesses correctly, he gets to eat the worm.
- The game continues with the worm keeper becoming the pigeon, and another worm keeper is chosen.
- The game continues until each person has had the opportunity to be the pigeon.

Party Centers

Writing: Pigeon Dreams

What you will need: lined writing paper, pens and/or pencils.

- Remind guests of pigeon's dream of driving the bus in the book *Don't Let the Pigeon Drive the Bus* by Mo Willems.
- Ask guests to think of something they dream of doing in the future.
- Ask them to write about their dream and the steps they will take to make it happen.

Science: Animal Nightlife

What you will need: photographs of a variety of animals. (Some of the animals will need to be nocturnal.) Old magazines are a great source for these photographs.

Remind guests how the pigeon did not want to go to sleep in the book *Don't Let the Pigeon Stay Up Late* by Mo Willems.

When your group is ready:

- Explain what nocturnal means and share specific examples of nocturnal animals.
- Ask guests to sort out which animals are nocturnal and which are not from the pictures.

Math: My Favorite Dog

What you will need: pictures of different dog breeds, access to a chalkboard or wipe-off board.

Remind your guests about how the pigeon wanted a puppy in the book *The Pigeon Wants a Puppy* by Mo Willems.

When your group is ready, give the following directions:

- Look at the pictures of the different breeds of dogs.
- One at a time, vote on which breed is your favorite.
- Graph all of the answers on the chalkboard or wipe-off board.
- Once the graph is complete ask them which breed was most popular and which breed was least popular.

Technology

Mo Willem's Pigeon has his own Web site full of fun activities: http://www.pigeon presents.com/.

*Guests can learn more about author Mo Willems and his other books on his Web site: http://www.mowillems.com/.

*The Cornell Lab of Orinthology has a great site dedicated to facts about pigeons and pigeon watching: http://www.birds.cornell.edu/pigeonwatch.

Party Snack

Hot Dogs

What you will need: hot dogs, hot dog buns, mustard, ketchup, relish, tongs to put the hot dogs on the buns, plates, spoons, napkins.

I recommend cooking the hot dogs ahead of time and keeping them warm in a crock pot.

When your group is ready, demonstrate and give the following directions:

- Remind guests about the book *The Pigeon Finds a Hot Dog* by Mo Willems.
- Place the hot dog on the bun and dress it with your favorite toppings. Eat up!

8

Socks Rock

Featured Books

Fox in Socks by Dr. Seuss
Timothy Cox Will Not Change His Socks by Robert Kinerk
New Socks by Bob Shea
10 Little Sock Monkeys by Harriet Ziefert
*Where Will This Shoe Take You? by Laurie Lawlor

Where Will This Shoe Take You? by Laurie Lawlor is a chapter book with lots of text. Most of the text revolves around the history of shoes, but there are a few sections that cover the history of socks and how they have evolved over time. It might be fun to share some of this history during your story time.

Invite guests to wear their favorite pair of socks to this party.

Party Game

Sock Hop

Instead of a traditional game, turn on the music to start this party. Give your guests the opportunity to dance off some energy before your story time begins.

Party Centers

*Writing: My Socks Rock

This activity celebrates the book *New Socks* by Bob Shea.
What you will need: lined writing paper, pens and/or pencils.

When your group is ready, give the following directions:

- Imagine that you have a new pair of socks that will give you special talents or skills.
- Write about your new socks and new talents.

Vocabulary: Rhyme Time

This activity celebrates the book *Fox in Socks* by Dr. Seuss.
What you will need: index cards, marker.

Before your guests arrive:

- Find all of the rhyming pairs of words in the book *Fox in Socks* by Dr. Seuss. Write one word on each card.
- Begin this center by talking about what rhyming words are and how they sound the same.

Remind your guests about all of the rhyming words in the book *Fox in Socks* by Dr. Seuss.

When your group is ready, give the following directions:

- Match each word on a card with another word that it rhymes with.
- This center is complete when every word has a rhyming mate.

Art: Sock Puppets

This activity celebrates the book *10 Little Sock Monkeys* by Harriet Ziefert.
What you will need: one large clean sock for each guest, yarn in various colors, glue, scissors, and markers.

When your group is ready, demonstrate and give the following directions:

- Make a sock creature from the supplies listed earlier.
- Encourage guests to draw faces and use the yarn as hair.
- Show them how the sock creatures can be puppets.

Math: Sock Sort

What you will need: a basket full of clean socks in various colors and sizes.

- Ask guests to sort the socks by color and size.
- Ask guests the following questions:

  How many pairs do you have of each color?

  What color do you have the most of?

  What color do you have the least of?

  How many large pairs do you have?

  How many medium size pairs do you have?

  How many small pairs do you have?

*Technology

Enjoy lots of different interactive games in Seussville: http://www.seussville.com/.

Read a brief history of socks here: http://www.lonelysock.com/SockHistory.html.

*Party Snack

Sugar Cookie Socks

What you will need: a pre-made sugar cookie in the shape of a sock for each guest. (You could use a Christmas stocking-shaped cookie cutter to make this shape.) You will also need frosting, an assortment of cookie decorations, plates, plastic knives, and napkins.

When your group is ready, demonstrate and give the following directions:

- Spread frosting on the cookie.
- Create a unique sock with the decorations provided.

9

Moonlight Madness

Featured Books

Goodnight Moon by Margaret Wise Brown
Kitten's First Full Moon by Kevin Henkes
Owl Moon by Jane Yolen
Papa, Please Get the Moon for Me by Eric Carle
*Faces of the Moon by Bob Crelin

Party Game

Hot Moon

What you will need: an inflatable beach ball or some other kind of large, bouncy ball, music.

Gather your guests in a circle. Begin by explaining that during the day, the temperature on the moon can get well above 200 degrees. In this game, your group will pretend like this ball is the moon.

When your group is ready, give the following directions:

- Just like in the classic game, Hot Potato, you will pass you moon around the circle quickly until the music stops.
- Whoever has the moon when the music stops is eliminated from play.
- The person left standing at the end of all rounds played wins!

Party Centers

*Writing: All I Need Is Hope

What you will need: lined writing paper, pens, or pencils.

- Begin this activity by re-reading the final page of *Owl Moon* by Jane Yolen.
- Point out the word *hope* and define it.
- Ask each guest to come up with one thing that they hope for.
- Ask them to write down what it is and why they hope for it.

Math: Mouse Hunt

What you will need: a copy of *Goodnight Moon* by Margaret Brown.

- Each spread of this book that shows the room has the mouse in a different place.
- Ask guests to practice critical thinking and problem solving skills by searching for and finding the mouse in each spread.

Art/Science: Moon Faces

What you will need: paper plates, gray crayons or markers, a copy of the book *Faces of the Moon* by Bob Crelin.

Remind guests about the different phases of the moon presented in the book *Faces of the Moon* by Bob Crelin and *Papa, Please Get the Moon for Me* by Eric Carle.

When your group is ready, demonstrate and give the following directions:

- Ask guests to choose their favorite moon phase and replicate it using the paper plate and gray crayon.
- Demonstrate how to fold the paper plate to get the different crescents, half moon and full moon shapes.
- Show guests how to shade the moon as it is illustrated in *Faces of the Moon* by Bob Crelin.

*Technology

View photographs of the different moon phases at: http://tycho.usno.navy.mil/vphase.html.

Learn more about the phases of the moon at: http://www.harcourtschool.com/activity/moon_phases/.

*Party Snack

*Milkshakes

What you will need: chocolate, vanilla, and strawberry ice cream: blender; ice cream scoop; cups; straws; and napkins.

In honor of *Kitten's First Full Moon* by Kevin Henkes, invite your guests to make and enjoy milkshakes.

When your group is ready, demonstrate and give the following directions:

- Choose an ice cream flavor.
- Place two scoops into the blender for each shake.
- Blend until it is a smooth drinkable consistency.
- Poor into a cup and serve with a straw.

10

Barnyard Blowout

Featured Books

Click, Clack, Moo: Cows That Type by Doreen Cronin
Duck on a Bike by David Shannon
Picnic Farm by Christine Morton
Baby Farm Animals by Merrill Windsor
The Milk Makers by Gail Gibbons

Party Game

Bicycle Fun

This activity celebrates the book *Duck on a Bike* by David Shannon. This activity will need to be done outside or in a large gymnasium.
What you will need: two–three bicycles and orange cones.

Before your guests arrive:

- Set up a bicycle course with the orange cones.

When your group is ready:

- Explain the course to your guests.
- Give each person an opportunity to ride through it.

Party Centers

Writing and Technology: Letter Writing

What you will need: computers, word processors, or typewriters.
This activity celebrates the book *Click, Clack, Moo: Cows That Type* by Doreen Cronin.

When your group is ready:

- Remind your guests how the cows communicated to the farmer what they wanted by typing letters to him.
- Ask guests to type a letter to a parent, teacher, or friend requesting something.
- Provide three–four sentences explaining why they need what they are asking for.

Science: Milking a Cow

This activity celebrates *The Milk Makers* by Gail Gibbons.
What you will need: index cards, marker.

Before your guests arrive:

- Write each of these steps on its own index card with a marker:
    1. A dairy cow is milked by hand or with a milking machine.
    2. The milk is moved to a cooling tank.
    3. The milk is pumped into the tank of a truck.
    4. The milk is shipped to a dairy.
    5. The milk is tested and cleaned.
    6. The milk is pasteurized and homogenized.
    7. The milk is packaged and dated.
    8. Trucks deliver the milk to the store.
- Mix the cards up out of order.

When your group is ready, give the following directions:

- Order the milk-making steps correctly.
- You may want to have a copy of the book at the center so that guests can check their work.

Vocabulary: Baby Animal Names

What you will need: index cards, marker.
This activity celebrates the book *Baby Farm Animals* by Merrill Windsor.

Before your guests arrive:

- Write each of the following words on its own index card:
  pig, piglet, cow, calf, horse, foal, hen, chick, goat, kid, goose, gosling.
- Mix the cards up in random order.

When your group is ready, give the following directions:

- Match the correct animal with its corresponding baby animal name.

*Technology

Enjoy a variety of farm games at www.farm-games.com.
Learn more about farms and farm animals at www.kidsfarm.com/farm.htm.

Party Snack

*Potluck Picnic

This activity celebrates the book *Picnic Farm* by Christine Morton.

Assign each guest to bring one of the following foods: deviled eggs, plums, bread, butter, honey, and chocolate cake.

What you will need: paper plates, plastic forks and knives, and napkins

- Before sitting down to enjoy these potluck treats, remind guests that these different foods came from the farm and were featured in the book *Picnic Farm* by Christine Morton.

11

Awesome Autumn

Featured Books

Pumpkin Fair by Eve Bunting
Red Leaf, Yellow Leaf by Lois Ehlert
There Was an Old Lady Who Swallowed a Pie by Alison Jackson
Milly and the Macy's Parade by Shana Corey
We Gather Together by Wendy Pfeffer

Party Game

Costume Parade

This activity celebrates the book *Milly and the Macy's Parade* by Shana Corey.

- Instead of a game, begin this celebration with a parade.
- Since autumn is often a time of costumes and dress-up, encourage your guests to come to this party in costume.
- If it is a nice day, parade around the outside of your building. If the weather is not cooperative, parade around the inside of your building.

Party Centers

Writing: A Time for Thanksgiving

This activity celebrates the book *We Gather Together* by Wendy Pfeffer.
What you will need: lined paper and pens or pencils.

- Remind guests of what they learned in the book regarding the harvest season being a time of thanksgiving.
- Ask your guests to make a list of all of the people and things that they are grateful for.

Art: Pumpkin Pals

This activity celebrates the book *Pumpkin Fair* by Eve Bunting.

What you will need: a small pumpkin for each guest, tempera paints in a variety of colors, paint brushes, old newspaper (for table coverings), and smocks to protect clothing.

When your group is ready, demonstrate and give the following directions:

- Remind your guests of all of the different pumpkins featured in the book *Pumpkin Fair* by Eve Bunting.
- Use the paints and brushes to create a pumpkin pal.

*Science: Plant a Tree

This activity celebrates the book *Red Leaf, Yellow Leaf* by Lois Ehlert.
What you will need: tree sapling, small shovel, burlap strips, and a wooden stake.

- Following the directions in the back of *Red Leaf, Yellow Leaf*, plant a tree with your group.

*Math: Pumpkin Estimation

What you will need: a medium or large size pumpkin, scale, small pieces of paper, pencils, a basket or jar.

- Ask guests to practice their estimation skills by trying to guess how much the pumpkin weighs.
- Have them write their names and their guesses on pieces of paper to place in the basket or jar.
- Toward the end of your party, weigh the pumpkin on the scale.
- Look at all of the guesses and announce the name or names of the guests whose estimate came closest to the actual weight.

Technology

*Read about why leaves change color in the fall and engage in related fun activities at Science Made Simple: http://www.sciencemadesimple.com/leaves.html.

Choose your favorite fall symbol from this list and use their interactive painting tool to color it on the computer: http://www.apples4theteacher.com/coloring-pages/fall/.

*Party Snack

Pumpkin Pie

This snack celebrates the book *There Was an Old Lady Who Swallowed a Pie* by Alison Jackson.

Since this snack needs to chill for a couple of hours, you can either create it with your guests at the very beginning of your party to enjoy at the end, or you can make it yourself before the party and serve it to your guests.

What you will need:

1 envelope of Dream Whip topping

1 cup of canned pumpkin

2/3 cup of milk

1 package of vanilla instant pudding

$^3/_4$ teaspoon of pumpkin pie spice

1 prebaked pie shell

When your group is ready:

- Prepare Dream Whip topping as directed on the envelope.
- Set aside 1 cup to garnish with.
- Add pumpkin, milk, pudding, and spice to remaining Dream Whip.
- Beat slowly until blended (about one minute).
- Pour into pie shell and chill for two hours.
- Garnish with leftover topping. Enjoy!

12

Winter Whirligig

> ### Featured Books
>
> *The Snowy Day* by Ezra Jack Keats
> **Snowflake Bentley* by Jacqueline Briggs Martin
> *The Mitten* by Jan Brett
> *The Snowman* by Raymond Briggs
> *Snowballs* by Lois Ehlert

Party Game

Frosty Friend

This game celebrates *The Snowman* by Raymond Briggs.
What you will need: a roll of toilet paper, a hat, and construction paper in a variety of colors for each team.

When your group is ready:

- Divide your guests into teams of four–five.
- When you say, GO, they should wrap one of their team members in toilet paper, place the hat on his or her head and use the construction paper to make eyes, nose, buttons, etc.
- Teams need to work fast. At the end of 15 minutes, each team can debut their new frosty friend.

Party Centers

Writing: Your Favorite Way to Spend a Snow Day

This activity celebrates *The Snowy Day* by Ezra Jack Keats.
What you will need: lined writing paper and pens or pencils.

- Begin this activity by reminding guests about Peter's day in the snow.
- Ask your guests to write a paragraph describing their favorite way to spend a snowy day.

Science: Picturing Snowflakes

What you will need: a bucket of snow, small spoon, two–three microscopes and slides, drawing paper, and pencils.

Begin this activity by explaining that guests will observe, record, and enjoy snow the way Wilson Bentley did in the book *Snowflake Bentley* by Jacqueline Briggs Martin.

When your group is ready, demonstrate and give the following directions:

- Spoon a tiny bit of snow onto a slide.
- Place it under the microscope.
- Draw pictures of the snow crystals observed.

Reading Comprehension: Ordering Animals

What you will need: lined writing paper, pencils, a copy of the book *The Mitten* by Jan Brett.

- Ask guests to try to make a list of all of the animals that hid inside of the mitten in the book *The Mitten* by Jan Brett.
- Try to list the animals in the order in which they entered the mitten.
- Encourage guests to use the book if they get stuck or want to check their work.

Art: Snow Friend

This activity celebrates the books *The Snowman* by Raymond Briggs and *Snowballs* by Lois Ehlert.

What you will need: three tin cans for each guest—one large, one medium, and one small (these cans need to still have the food in them); white construction paper cut into strips to fit around each size can; markers; scissors; glue; tape; glitter; yarn; buttons; and pipe cleaners.

When your group is ready, demonstrate and give the following directions:

- Wrap the construction paper around each can and secure it with a piece of tape.
- Stack the cans with the largest on the bottom, medium-sized in the middle, and small one on top like the shape of a snowman.
- Use all of the craft supplies to decorate the snow friend.
- After displaying the snow friends for a week or two, remove the construction paper from each can and donate the cans of food to a local food pantry.

Technology

Guests will enjoy a host of activities and games for *The Mitten* and all of Jan Brett's other books on her Web site: http://www.janbrett.com/.

Observe wildlife and signs of winter at the National Wildlife Federation site for kids: http://www.nwf.org/Kids/Your-Big-Backyard/Fun/Outdoors/Observing -Wildlife/Signs-of-Winter.aspx.

Party Snack

Popcorn Balls

Use the recipe in the back of the book *Snowballs* by Lois Ehlert to create this yummy snack.

13

Spring Up a Story!

Featured Books

The Tiny Seed by Eric Carle
It's Spring! by Else Holmelund Minarik
The Boy Who Didn't Believe in Spring by Lucille Clifton
Red Rubber Boot Day by Mary Lyn Ray
What Happens in Spring? by Sara L. Latta

Party Game

Leap for Spring

This activity celebrates the book *It's Spring!* by Else Holmelund Minarik. Celebrate spring like our cat friends with a leap frog race.

- This activity is best played outside or in a large gymnasium.
- Pair each guest with a partner and line them up at the starting line.
- Demonstrate with a partner how to leap frog over each other.
- When you say, "Go," your guests leap frog to the finish line.
- The first pair to make it to the line, win!

Party Centers

Writing: Signs of Spring

This activity celebrates the book *The Boy Who Didn't Believe in Spring* by Lucille Clifton. What you will need: lined writing paper and pens or pencils.

- Ask guests to write about all of the things they would see, hear, smell, touch, and taste in spring.

Science: Make a Rainbow

This activity celebrates the books *Red Rubber Boot Day* by Mary Lyn Ray and *What Happens in Spring?* by Sara L. Latta.

What you will need: a baking pan filled with one–two inches of water, small mirror, and a sunny window.

When your group is ready, demonstrate and give the following directions:

- Place the pan of water in the sunny window.
- Dip the mirror into the water, and hold it so that the sun reflects on it.
- Move the mirror.
- You should soon see a rainbow on the ceiling.

Art: Sunflower Faces

This activity celebrates the book *The Tiny Seed* by Eric Carle.

What you will need: paper plate, yellow construction paper, yellow tissue paper, brown markers, green construction paper, scissors, glue.

Before your guests arrive:

- Cut a circle from the yellow construction paper the size of the paper plate for each guest. This will be the face.
- Cut several rectangular strips from the yellow tissue paper for each guest. These will be the petals.
- Cut a long rectangular stem and a few small rectangular leaves from the green construction paper.

When your guests arrive, demonstrate and give the following directions:

- Glue the yellow face to the paper plate and the petals around the outside.
- Glue the stem to the bottom of the plate.
- Attach the leaves to the stem.
- Draw eyes, nose, and mouth with the brown marker on the sunflower face.

Technology

Engage in games and activities and learn more about Earth and spring at: http://www.eo.ucar.edu/kids/index.html.

Track spring's journey north here: http://www.learner.org/jnorth/spring2005/index.html.

Party Snack

Rays of Sunshine

What you will need: refrigerator biscuits, apple jelly, kitchen scissors, plates, napkins, baking sheet.

When your group is ready, demonstrate and give the following directions:

- Place biscuits on baking sheet, leaving plenty of space between each.
- Cut the edges halfway to the center into strips to create the rays.
- Bake according to package directions.
- Let cool for 10 minutes.
- Spread apple jelly onto each biscuit and enjoy!

14

Summer Jubilee

Featured Books

Night at the Fair by Donald Crews
One Hot Summer Day by Nina Crews
Louie's Goose by H.M. Ehrlich
The Fabulous Firework Family by James Flora
What Happens in Summer? by Sara L. Latta

Party Game

Bean Bag Toss

Celebrate the book *Night at the Fair* by Donald Crews by playing a classic carnival game.

What you will need: five bean bags, five small pails.

- Line the pails up in one row with about a foot of space between each one.
- Line your guests up behind the pails.
- Each guest will try to toss one bean bag into each pail.
- Those who make all five pails win the game.
- It might be nice to provide small carnival prizes for the winners.

Party Centers

Writing: Problem Solving

This activity celebrates the book *Louie's Goose* by H. M. Ehrlich.
What you will need: lined writing paper, pens and/or pencils.

- Remind your guests how Louie's parents had helped him fix many of his problems and how he was eventually able to fix Louie all by himself.
- Explain that parents and teachers are always there to help solve tough problems, but that children can solve some problems on their own.
- Share a few examples.
- Ask guests to write about a problem they had and the steps they took to solve it.

Math: Chalking Up Sums and Differences

This activity celebrates the book *One Hot Summer Day* by Nina Crews. What you will need: sidewalk chalk and game dice.

- This activity will need to be done outside.
- Give each guest a few pieces of chalk and a pair of dice.
- Roll the dice.
- Make an addition problem from the two numbers that they roll.
- Write the number sentence on the sidewalk and solve.
- After several rounds of addition, switch over to subtraction.

Art: Fantastic Fireworks

This activity celebrates the book *The Fabulous Firework Family* by James Flora. What you will need: construction paper, pencils, glue, glitter, paper plates.

When your group is ready, demonstrate and give the following directions:

- Draw several firework shapes on the paper with the pencil. Get inspired by the shapes of the fireworks you saw in the book.
- Trace your pencil shapes with a thin line of glue.
- Sprinkle a small amount of glitter in a variety of colors over your shapes.
- Softly tap your paper over a paper plate to remove any excess glitter.

Science: Fun with the Sun

This activity celebrates the book *What Happens in Summer?* by Sara L. Latta. What you will need: two shallow bowls, water, thermometer.

- Fill each bowl with an inch of water.
- Place one bowl in direct sunlight.
- Place one bowl in the shade.
- Check the temperatures of both bowls.
- Let the bowls sit for an hour or so.
- Check the temperatures again.
- Ask the following questions:

Are the temperatures the same? Is one bowl warmer than the other? If so, why?

*Technology

Let your class learn all about the weather that comes with different seasons through games, maps and activities with this fun fact-filled Web site: http://www.theweatherchannelkids.com/

Learn more about the summer solstice here: http://news.nationalgeographic.com/news/2010/06/100621-summer-solstice-2010-first-day-of-summer-longest-year-science/

Party Snack

*Freezer Pops

This snack celebrates the book *One Hot Summer Day* by Nina Crews

What you will need: Popsicle molds, presweetened lemonade mix, water, napkins, access to a freezer.

- Stir the lemonade mix into the amount of water specified on the package.
- Pour into molds.
- Place in the freezer until frozen.
- Enjoy!

15

Garden Gala

Featured Books

Muncha! Muncha! Muncha! by Candace Fleming
Miss Rumphius by Barbara Cooney
Growing Vegetable Soup by Lois Ehlert
My First Garden by Tomek Bogacki
Grow It! by Erika Markmann

Grow It! by Erika Markmann has a lot of text. You may want to opt to only read some important highlights and share some of the delightful illustrations.

Party Game

Bunny, Bunny, Run!

This game celebrates the book *Muncha! Muncha! Muncha!* by Candace Fleming. This game is played just like the classic *Duck, Duck, Goose* except that the goal here is to catch the bunny who has been snacking in your garden.

- Gather your group in a circle and have them sit.
- Choose a gardener.
- The gardener will walk around the circle, softly tapping the head of each bunny saying, "Bunny, Bunny, Bunny," . . . etc.
- When he reaches the bunny he wants to chase, the gardener will tap that bunny on the head and say, "Run!"
- The gardener and bunny will run around the circle trying to beat the other back to the spot where the bunny was seated.
- Now the bunny will get a chance to be gardener.
- The game continues until each guest has had the opportunity to be the gardener and/or bunny.

Party Centers

Writing: A Beautiful World

This activity celebrates the book *Miss Rumphius* by Barbara Cooney.
What you will need: lined writing paper, pens and/or pencils.

- Remind your guests how *Miss Rumphius* made the world a more beautiful place.
- Discuss other ways to make the world more beautiful.
- Ask your guests to write a paragraph or two describing how they would go about making the world more beautiful.

Science: Salad Container Gardening

This activity celebrates the books *My First Garden* by Tomek Bogacki and *Grow It!* by Erika Markmann.

What you will need: seed packets of lettuce, tomatoes, and cucumbers; potting soil; small shovels; containers for planting; drill; water.

Before your guests arrive:

- Drill drainage holes in the bottom of your containers.

When your group is ready:

- Pour potting soil into containers.
- Plant seeds. Be sure to follow directions on the package for depth of planting and distance from surrounding plants.
- Place some soil on top of the seeds.
- Water the garden.
- Place in a well lit area.
- Water and weed regularly, and soon you and your class will enjoy a salad full of veggies you grew yourselves.

Art: Tissue Paper Flowers

This activity celebrates the books *Miss Rumphius* by Barbara Cooney and *My First Garden* by Tomek Bogacki.

What you will need: construction paper, pencils, small pieces of tissue paper in a variety of colors, glue.

When your group is ready, demonstrate and give the following directions:

- Using the pencil, draw a large flower on the paper.
- Place a piece of tissue paper around your finger, forming a small cup.
- Place a dab of glue on the bottom of the cupped tissue and place it somewhere on your flower.
- Fill in your entire flower outline with the colorful tissue paper pieces.

*Technology

Learn all about gardening and participate in many activities on this Web site: http://www.kidsgardening.com/

My First Garden: http://urbanext.illinois.edu/firstgarden/

Find links to many gardening ideas for kids at this Web site: http://www
.lillydunn.com/

Party Snack

Vegetable Soup

This snack celebrates the book *Growing Vegetable Soup* by Lois Ehlert.
The back of the book *Growing Vegetable Soup* contains a complete list of ingredients and directions to make a delicious pot of vegetable soup.

16

Back to School Blast

Featured Books

The Kissing Hand by Audrey Penn
We Share Everything by Robert Munsch
Show and Tell Bunnies by Kathryn Lasky
The Day the Teacher Went Bananas by James Howe
Hooway for Wodney Wat by Helen Lester
*Hopscotch, Hangman, Hot Potato, and Ha Ha Ha by Jack Maguire

Note: *Hopscotch, Hangman, Hot Potato, and Ha Ha Ha* by Jack Maguire is a chapter book full of classic games played in the classroom and out on the playground. It is not a book to be read cover-to-cover during story time. However, I encourage you to scan the different activities and choose a few to implement into your back-to-school blast.

Party Game

*Jump Rope

What you will need: several jump ropes.
Take turns practicing each of these jump rope variations:

- Jump with two feet.
- Jump on one foot.
- Take big jumps.
- Take small jumps.
- Jump fast.
- Jump slow.
- Line your guests up and have a jump rope race.

In honor of the book *Hooway for Wodney Wat* by Helen Lester, play a game of Simon Says.

Party Centers

Show and Tell

This activity celebrates the book *Show and Tell Bunnies* by Kathryn Lasky.

- Before the party, ask your guests to bring something that is special to them for show and tell.
- When your group is ready, practice communication and public speaking skills by giving each person a turn to show what they have brought and to tell what it is and why it is special to them.

*Writing: To Share or Not to Share

This activity celebrates the book *We Share Everything* by Robert Munsch.
What you will need: lined writing paper, pens and/or pencils.

When your group is ready:

- Share a few examples of when it is good to share. Examples might include working a puzzle together, building something with blocks, taking turns at a favorite center, bringing treats to share on a special occasion.
- Discuss what germs are and how they are spread.
- Share some examples of what is not good to share. Examples might include: tissues, eating from the same utensils, and drinking from the same cup, etc.
- Ask guests to write one example of when it is good to share and why, or one example of when it is not a good idea to share and why.

Art: Hands of Love

This activity celebrates the book *The Kissing Hand* by Audrey Penn.
What you will need: construction paper, pencils, markers.

When your group is ready, demonstrate and give the following directions:

- Use the pencil to trace both of your hands on the construction paper.
- Go over the outline of your hands with a marker.
- Write at least two things that you love about your parent(s) in the center of each hand.

*Technology

Find lots of different back-to-school coloring sheets on the following Web sites: http://www.coloring.ws/school1.htm; http://www.preschoolcoloringbook.com/color/cpback.shtml; and http://www.activityvillage.co.uk/back_to_school_coloring _pages_links.htm.

Party Snack

*Banana Split

This snack celebrates the book *The Day the Teacher Went Bananas* by James Howe.

What you will need: vanilla ice cream, bananas (split in half), whipped topping, a variety of sauces (caramel, fudge, strawberry), a variety of toppings (chocolate candies, gummy snacks, etc.) cherries, bowls, spoons, napkins, ice cream scoop.

When your group is ready:

- Place one banana open-faced in each bowl.
- Place one scoop of ice cream into each bowl.
- Let your guests top their banana splits with their favorite sauces and toppings.

17

Pirate Party

Featured Books

Do Pirates Take Baths? by Kathy Tucker
Captain Abdul's Little Treasure by Colin McNaughton
Tough Boris by Mem Fox
Rabbit Pirates: A Tale of the Spinach Main by Judy Cox
*Pirates: Robbers of the High Seas by Gail Gibbons

Party Game

Treasure Hunt

What you will need: pencil, paper, prizes, and container for the treasure.
Note: Small pieces of candy might make good prizes for this game.

Before your guests arrive:

• Write clues leading from clue to clue and eventually leading to the treasure.
• Put the treasure in its hiding place and place the clues where they belong around the room.

When your group is ready:

• Read the first clue.
• Let your group figure out the answer to the clue that leads to the next clue.
• The game continues like this until they have found the treasure (prizes).

Party Centers

Vocabulary: Making a French Connection

This activity celebrates the book *Rabbit Pirates: A Tale of the Spinach Main* by Judy Cox.
What you will need: a copy of this book.

• As you read this book, ask your guests if they can figure out the meanings of the French words used throughout the book by the way the words are used in each sentence.

- If you need any help, there is a French glossary of terms at the beginning of the book.

Writing: When Pirates Cry

This activity celebrates the book *Tough Boris* by Mem Fox.
What you will need: lined writing paper, pens and/or pencils.

- Begin this activity by discussing different kinds of feelings.
- Remind your group how Boris got very sad and cried.
- Share some situations in your own life when you have cried. If you have other adults at your party, ask them to share examples, too.
- Ask your group to write about a time that they experienced sadness and/or pain and cried.

Math: Dividing Up Treasure

This activity celebrates the book *Captain Abdul's Little Treasure* by Colin McNaughton.
What you will need: 12 small pieces of candy, a piece of paper, marker.

- Begin by reminding your guests how the pirates taught the baby how to divide up a treasure.
- Explain that your group will learn how to divide up a treasure, too.
- Lay out the pieces of candy.
- Ask your group how to divide the twelve pieces of candy evenly between four people.
- Demonstrate by drawing four circles on the paper.
- Place one piece of candy in each circle. Repeat until the candy is gone.
- Point out how we now have four groups of candy with three pieces in each group.
- Repeat this exercise dividing the candy between three friends and then between two friends.

Art/Geography: Treasure Maps

This activity celebrates the book *Pirates: Robbers of the High Seas* by Gail Gibbons.
What you will need: medium sized paper bags, scissors, and colored pencils.

Before your group arrives:

- Cut the front and back faces from each paper sack so that each side rests flat on the table. Each guest will use one face for their project.

When your group is ready, demonstrate and give the following directions:

- Begin by reminding guests about the treasure maps we learned about in the book.
- Share example pictures from the book and other pictures if you can find them.

- Ask guests to use the colored pencils to draw their own treasure maps.
- Demonstrate how to wad the map up into a ball and then flatten it back out. It should now look like an old treasure map.

*Technology

Read about pirates and play pirate games at the National Geographic Web site: http://www.nationalgeographic.com/pirates/.

Play games and have fun at a Web site dedicated to the book *Treasure Island* by Robert Louis Stevenson: http://www.ukoln.ac.uk/services/treasure/.

*Party Snack: Fish Fruit Snacks and Crackers

We learn in the book *Do Pirates Take Baths?* by Kathy Tucker that pirates eat things like cod and barnacle stew. Serve your little pirates a mixture of fish-shaped snack crackers and fish-shaped gummy fruit snacks.

18

Birthday Extravaganza

Featured Books

It's My Birthday by Pat Hutchins
Birthday Zoo by Deborah Lee Rose
Happy Birthday, Jesse Bear by Nancy White Carlstrom
Benjamin's 365 Birthdays by Judi Barrett
*Celebrations: Festivals, Carnivals, and Feast Days from around the World by Barnabas and
  Anabel Kindersley

Note: *Celebrations* has a lot of text. You will only want to share the few pages of text and illustrations that are devoted to birthdays from around the world.

Party Game

Birthday Balloon Pop

What you will need: several balloons, whistle, and stop watch.

Before your guests arrive:

- Blow up all of the balloons
- Place them all around the room.

When your group is ready:

- When you blow the whistle, your group will have two minutes to find and pop as many balloons as they can.
- Guests may only use their own body parts to pop the balloons (hands, feet, bottoms, etc.) They may not use any objects to pop the balloons.

Party Centers

*Writing: Sharing Your Special Day

This activity celebrates the book *It's My Birthday* by Pat Hutchins.
What you will need: lined writing paper, pens and/or pencils.

When your group is ready, ask them to think about how they share their birthdays with others.

- Ask them to think about the following questions:

  Do you share cake or other treats?

  Do you play games together?

  Do you sing together?

  Do you share your gifts?

  Do you have other birthday traditions that you share?

- Ask your group to write a paragraph or two describing all the ways in which they share their special day with others.

*Science: Petting Zoo

This activity celebrates the book *Birthday Zoo* by Deborah Lee Rose.

Many birthdays are celebrated with a trip to the zoo or a petting zoo joining in the birthday party festivities.

- Invite your local zoo to bring a small group of animals to your party. Many zoos are happy to provide this educational service to local schools if they are contacted ahead of time and given plenty of notice.
- Ask the zookeeper to share some interesting facts about each animal.
- Give your guests the opportunity to ask questions.
- Give your guests the opportunity to pet and/or hold the animals when appropriate.

Math: Birthday Counting

What you will need: a copy of the book *Benjamin's 365 Birthdays* by Judi Barrett.

- After reading the book, remind your group how many days they have between birthdays.
- Practice counting with your group.
- Count by ones to 365.
- Count by fives to 365.

*Technology

Learn more about birthday traditions from around the world: http://www.birthdaycelebrations.net/traditions.htm.

Learn what famous people share your birthday: http://www.famousbirthdays.com/home.html.

Music: Birthday Cheer

Before you enjoy a cupcake, sing the cheer for birthdays at the end of the book *Happy Birthday, Jesse Bear* by Nancy White Calstrom. You may want to substitute the word "everyone" for "Jesse Bear."

Party Snack

*Birthday Cupcakes

What you will need: premade cupcakes, frosting, small candies, sprinkles and decors, paper plates, plastic knives, napkins.

When your group is ready, demonstrate and give the following directions:

- Spread frosting onto your cupcake.
- Decorate your cupcake with the candies, sprinkles, and decors.
- Enjoy!

19

Family Fun Night

Featured Books

Julius: The Baby of the World by Kevin Henkes
I Love You Like Crazy Cakes by Rose Lewis
Mama's Coming Home by Kate Banks
Song and Dance Man by Karen Ackerman
Daddy Makes the Best Spaghetti by Anna Grossnickle Hines
Celebrating Families by Rosemarie Hausherr

Party Game

Tap Dance Fever

This activity celebrates the book *The Song and Dance Man* by Karen Ackerman.
What you will need: a CD of Vaudeville music, CD player.
Instead of playing a traditional game, turn up the music. Dance and celebrate Vaudeville.

Party Centers

Writing: Home Sweet Home

This activity celebrates the book *Mama's Coming Home* by Kate Banks.
What you will need: lined writing paper, pens and/or pencils.

When your group is ready, give the following directions:

- Think about a time that you were away from your family. Maybe you spent the night with a friend, a weekend with Grandma and Grandpa or maybe you went away to camp?
- Think about how you felt when you were able to come home.
- Write about how you felt.

Art: Family Portrait

What you will need: construction paper, markers.

When your group is ready, explain the following:

- In the book *Julius: The Baby of the World* by Kevin Henkes, we see Lilly draw a portrait of her family.
- Use the construction paper and markers to draw a portrait of your family.
- Label each person with their name.

Social Studies: Where We Are From

This activity celebrates the books *I Love You like Crazy Cakes* by Rose Lewis and *Celebrating Families* by Rosemarie Hausherr.

What you will need: world maps, globes, encyclopedias.

When your group is ready, demonstrate and give the following directions:

- Begin by defining ancestors.
- Ask parents to share with their children where their ancestors came from.
- Find this place or these places on a map or globe.
- Look the country up in an encyclopedia.
- Find three interesting facts to share about each country.

Technology

*Build a family tree: http://pbskids.org/wayback/family/tree/index.html.

Enjoy fun and games with Lilly and Julius and the rest of the mice on Kevin Henkes' official Web site: http://www.kevinhenkes.com/young.asp.

Party Snack

Super Simple Spaghetti

This snack celebrates the book *Daddy Makes the Best Spaghetti* by Anna Grossnickle Hines.

What you will need: one pound spaghetti noodles, one 26-ounce jar of marinara, grated parmesan cheese, strainer, large pot to cook the spaghetti, slotted spaghetti spoon, plates, plastic knives and forks, napkins.

- Boil the spaghetti according to package directions.
- Drain the spaghetti.
- Pour spaghetti back into pot.
- Add marinara.
- Cook on low, stirring until heated through.
- Serve on plates.
- Add parmesan to taste.

Note: You can prepare this dish during the party with the help of your guests or prepare it ahead of time. You could also ask your guests to contribute sides like salad, bread, drinks, dessert, etc.

20

Rain Rumpus

Featured Books

Come On, Rain! by Karen Hesse
*Cloudy With a Chance of Meatballs by Judi Barrett
The Puddle by David McPhail
The Cat in the Hat by Dr. Seuss
*A Rainy Day by Sandra Markle

Party Game

Rain Dance

This activity celebrates the book *Come On, Rain!* by Karen Hesse.
Note: This is an outdoor activity.
What you will need: sprinkler, hose, access to water outside where you can attach to hose.

- Celebrate rain and this book by turning on the sprinkler and letting your guests pretend that they are running and playing in the rain.

Party Centers

**Writing: Rainy Day Fun*

This activity celebrates the book *The Cat in the Hat* by Dr. Seuss.
What you will need: lined writing paper, pens and/or pencils.

- Ask your guests to write about all of the fun things they could do on a rainy day.

Art: It's Raining What?

This activity celebrates the book *Cloudy With a Chance of Meatballs* by Judi Barrett.
What you will need: drawing paper, colored pencils.

- Remind your guests of all of the different foods that fell from the sky in the book.
- Ask your group to imagine odd things other than food falling from the sky.
- Ask them to draw a picture of the sky raining down their strange objects.

*Science: Puddle Float Fun

This activity celebrates the book *The Puddle* by David McPhail.

What you will need: plastic bin filled with water, three–four objects that will float, three–four objects that will not float.

- Begin by explaining that your group will be testing objects to see if they float.
- Ask your group to make predictions about which items will float and which items will sink.
- Ask your group to test each object by setting it in the puddle.
- Evaluate results. Which objects floated? Which objects did not? How close were the actual results to the predicted results?

Technology

Have fun visiting Seussville: http://www.seussville.com/lb/home.html.
*Learn more about the water cycle at this site: http://www.kidzone.ws/water/.
*Play weather games at this site: http://www.weatherwizkids.com/.

Party Snack

*Pancakes

This snack celebrates the book *Cloudy With a Chance of Meatballs* by Judi Barrett.

What you will need: precooked pancakes (found in the freezer section at the grocery store), syrup, butter, jelly, paper plates, plastic knives and forks, napkins.

- Heat the pancakes in a toaster or microwave oven.
- Place one–two on each plate.
- Encourage your guests to add their favorite toppings and enjoy!

21

Big Top Bash

Party Game

Circus Games

What you will need: inflated balloons, hula hoops, balance beam that sits low to the ground, circus music, CD player.

Turn on the music and encourage your guests to practice their big top circus skills:

- Try balancing a balloon on your nose.
- Jump through hoops.
- Practice acrobatic skills by walking on the balance beam.

Party Centers

*Writing: Circus Poem

This activity celebrates the book *Circus* by Charles Sullivan
What you will need: lined writing paper, pens and/or pencils.
Ask your guests to write their own poem about the circus.

Art: Painted Clowns

This activity celebrates the book *Last Night I Dreamed a Circus* by Maya Gottfried.
What you will need: pencils, white poster board, tempera paints, paintbrushes, paint shirts or smocks.

- Begin by sharing the beautiful circus paintings displayed in the book.
- Ask your guests to use their pencil to draw a clown face on the poster board. Remind them how different clown faces can be. They could be happy, sad, afraid, serious, etc.
- Get creative with paints and brushes. Ask them to paint their clown face portrait.

Math: Juggling Circus Subtraction

What you will need: seven small balls (foam, rubber or plastic will be best for this activity), paper, pencils.

Ask your guests to imagine that they are circus jugglers that keep dropping their balls.

Ask them to write number sentences for the following word problems:

- I juggle seven balls. Four drop. How many are left?
- I juggle four balls. Two drop. How many are left?
- I juggle six balls. Three drop. How many are left?
- I juggle five balls. Two drop. How many are left?
- I juggle four balls. One drops. How many are left?
- Ask your group to write the answers to their number sentences.
- They may use their juggling balls as counters.

*Technology

Learn more about the author of *Circus Family Dog*. Visit Andrew Clement's Web site. Read his biography, learn about his other books and enjoy his Fun Stuff section: http://www.andrewclements.com/index.html.

Play circus games at the official site of the Ringling Bros. Circus: http://www.ringling.com/.

Learn more about circus history: http://www.circushistory.org/.

Party Snack

*Circus Popcorn

What you will need: microwave popcorn, small paper sacks.

- Pop the popcorn according to package directions.
- Serve circus style in the small brown paper sacks.

22

Toy Show and Tell

Note: It might be a nice idea to ask your guests to bring a new or gently used toy to donate to a local charity.

Party Game

Show and Tell

Instead of a traditional party game, start this celebration by giving each guest the opportunity to show and tell about a favorite toy.

Party Centers

*Writing: Toy Giveaway

This activity celebrates the book *The Teddy Bear* by David McPhail.
What you will need: lined writing paper, pens and/or pencils.

- Begin by reminding your guests how the boy in the story decided to let the homeless man keep his teddy bear.
- Ask your guests to think about a time that they gave away one of their toys to a family member, friend, thrift shop, etc.
- Ask them to write about their special toy and how it made them feel to share the toy with someone else who could enjoy it as much as they did.

*Art: Toy Making (Light-Up Faces)

What you will need: pencils, paper lunch sacks, sheets of cellophane in a variety of colors, scissors, tape, flashlights.

Note: Small flashlights can be purchased at a dollar store. You could also ask parents to donate them.

When your group is ready, demonstrate and give the following directions:

- Use the pencil to draw a face on one side of the paper sack. Include eyes, nose, mouth, and eyebrows.
- Using the scissors, carefully cut out the eyes, nose, mouth, and eyebrows.
- Place a piece of cellophane over the face side of the bag. Cut it to fit the face.
- Tape the cellophane to the face.
- Place a flashlight inside the bag.
- When you turn on the flashlight, your face will glow.

*Science: Yo-Yo Science

This activity celebrates the book *Slim and Jim* by Richard Egielski.
What you will need: yo-yos, objects of varying size.

When your group is ready:

- Define gravity.
- Ask your group why the yo yo falls when we let go of it.
- Have your group drop other objects that are smaller, larger, lighter, and heavier.
- Compare the yo-yo and the other objects. Which object fell the fastest? Slowest?
- End this activity by letting your guests play with the yo-yos.

Technology

Have fun and play games at Disney's official site for *Toy Story 3*: http://disney.go.com/toystory/.

*A History of toys is found at http://www.britannica.com/EBchecked/topic/601284/toy/274906/History-of-toys.

Party Snack

Edible Play Dough

Note: Clean hands are important for all snack activities, but even more so for this one.

What you will need: 18-ounce jar of peanut butter, 6 tablespoons of honey, 1 ½ cups of powdered milk, paper plates.

- Mix ingredients until mixture is workable with hands.
- Let your guests play with their dough over their paper plates.
  - When they are finished playing, they may eat it.

23

Fishing Fun

Featured Books

Little Fish, Lost by Nancy Van Laan
BIG AL by Andrew Clements
A Million Fish . . . More or Less by Patricia C. McKissack
A House for Hermit Crab by Eric Carle
Sea Critters by Sylvia Earle
Down, Down, Down: A Journey to the Bottom of the Sea by Steve Jenkins

Party Game

Shell Hunt

What you will need: sandbox or sand table, seashells, buckets, shovels.
Note: You can make your own sandbox out of a cheap plastic child's swimming pool, or you could set rectangular shaped shallow plastic bins on top of tables to make your own sand table. Also, shells can be purchased inexpensively from most dollar stores.

- When you say, "Go," guests can start digging and hunting for seashell loot.
- After two minutes, stop the hunt.
- Everyone counts their shells. The person who finds the most shells wins.

Party Centers

Writing: Fish Friends

This activity celebrates the book *BIG AL* by Andrew Clements.
What you will need: lined writing paper, pens and/or pencils.

- Begin by reminding guests what a hard time BIG AL had making friends because of the way he looked.
- Ask your group to think about the qualities they would most like to have in a friend. Share some possible examples: kindness, honesty, generosity, loyalty, etc.
- Ask them to list these qualities in order of importance to them and write why each quality is important.

Art: Finger Painted Fish

This activity celebrates the book *Little Fish, Lost* by Nancy Van Laan.

What you will need: finger paints in many colors, paper, paint shirts and/or smocks.

- Begin by reminding your group about the different fish that Little Fish saw: striped, freckled, whiskered, puffy, etc.
- Ask your group to finger paint their own unique fish.

Math: Fishy Estimation

This activity celebrates the book *A Million Fish ... More or Less* by Patricia C. McKissack.

What you will need: a jar full of fish-shaped snack crackers or fish gummy snacks, small pieces of paper, pencils, basket.

- Ask your guests to estimate how many fish are in the jar.
- Have them write their name and guess on a small piece of paper and place it in the basket.
- The person who guesses closest to the actual amount wins the jar of fish.

*Technology

Go to these sites to learn some interesting fish facts: http://www.indianchild.com/fish.htm; http://www.iwrc-online.org/kids/Facts/Fish/fish.htm.

Party Snack

Under the Sea Dessert

What you will need: large clear bowl, blue Jell-O, gummy fish, plastic spoons, clear plastic cups, napkins.

- Prepare the Jell-O according to package directions.
- Stir in gummy fish.
- Chill in refrigerator.
- Serve in clear plastic cups.

24

Buggin' Out

Note: As guests arrive, have them work on this quick craft.

Give each child a bug bag (a paper lunch sack). Provide them with bug stamps to decorate their bag. They will be using these bags for a game later on.

Party Game

Caterpillar, Caterpillar, Butterfly!

This game is played just like Duck, Duck, Goose except that the child on the outside of the circle will chant "Caterpillar, caterpillar, caterpillar . . ." as he/she taps each guest's head lightly until they choose who will be *it*. When they tap that person, they will say, "Butterfly!" and the chase outside the circle will begin.

Party Centers

*Writing: If I Were a Bug

What you will need: lined writing paper, pens and/or pencils, drawing paper, colored pencils.

When your group is ready:

- Ask them to think about all of the bugs they saw in the books shared during story time.
- Ask them to think about what it would be like to be a bug, and if they were a bug, which kind of bug they would like to be.
- Ask them to write why they would like to be this kind of bug. Why is this bug so special?
- Follow-up by having them draw pictures of the bugs they chose.

Math: Sequencing

Eric Carle's *The Very Busy Spider* provides a great opportunity to practice sequencing and order.

What you will need: small plastic toy animals (one for each of the animals that speaks to Spider during the course of the book).

- Ask your group to line the animals up in the order in which they spoke to Spider in the story.
- A few extra copies of the book would be helpful to act as a reminder in case they get stuck or if they just want to check how much they actually remembered.

Science: Butterfly Release!

Prior to your Buggin' Out party, it would be great for you to order a butterfly kit. During the weeks leading up to the party, students can observe the life cycle changes until finally, a beautiful butterfly emerges from its cocoon. Your party would be a great time to release the butterfly into nature.

Art: Bug Collage

Much of Eric Carle's art is done with tissue paper collage. This center will provide guests with an opportunity to create their own collage.

What you will need: construction paper, various colors of tissue paper cut into small squares, pencils, glue.

- Ask students to draw an outline picture of their favorite bug on a piece of construction paper.
- Show them how to scrunch up the small squares of tissue paper and glue them around the lined edge and inside of their drawing until there is no space left uncovered.
- Showcase their art on a bulletin board.

*Technology

Log on to http://www.eric-carle.com/creativeprojects.html to view slide shows on how Eric Carle paints his tissue papers and how he creates his pictures. You could project this on to a large screen with power point and view as a group or set it up on individual computers for guests to view in small groups.

*Party Snack

Butterfly Bites

This snack celebrates the book *The Very Hungry Caterpillar* by Eric Carle.

What you will need: celery, cream cheese or peanut butter, raisins, large pretzel twists, and small pretzel sticks.

- Cut celery into three-inch pieces.
- Spread with cream cheese or peanut butter.
- Line the center with raisins.
- Attach a large pretzel twist to each side of the celery body like wings.
- Attach two small pretzels to the top of the body like antennae.
- Serve with any juice, but be sure to call it bug juice!

25

Dress-Up Day

Featured Books

Fancy Nancy by Jane O'Connor
Fancy Nancy, Bonjour Butterfly by Jane O'Connor
Fancy Nancy, Splendiforous Christmas by Jane O'Connor
Fancy Nancy and the Posh Puppy by Jane O'Connor
Costume by L. Rowland-Warne

Note: If there was ever a day for dress-up, this is it. Have your dress-up area stocked with ties, hats, bows, crowns, scarves, boas, sunglasses, and lots and lots of costume jewelry. As your guests arrive, encourage them try-on the fancy attire.

Note: *Costume* by L. Rowland-Warne is an Eyewitness book on the history and meaning of clothing. It is too long to read in its entirety during a story time. However, it is theme appropriate and will be of interest to older students. I suggest sharing a few highlights and many of the wonderful costume pictures.

Party Game

Word Hunt

Make a list of some of the fancy words found in the books on the wipe-of board ahead of time. Here is a short list of words you might use: exquisite, bonjour, exceptional, extraordinary, furious, elegant, gorgeous, aroma, heirlooms, delectable, and devastated

- After story time, ask your guests to look at the words on the board.
- Read the words together and talk about what they mean.
- Explain that you have hidden index cards around the room with these words written on them.
- When you say, "GO!" they will need to search the room and find as many words as possible.

Party Centers

Writing: I Like Your Style

This activity celebrates the book *Costume* by L. Rowland-Warne.

What you will need: lined writing paper, drawing paper, pens and/or pencils, colored pencils.

When your group is ready:

- Ask your group to think of someone who in their opinion has great style.
- You may want to share a few of examples from modern culture and/or style icons.
- Ask them to write about why they think this person's style is so special.
- Ask them to draw a picture of this person to show off their style.

Math: Bead Fun

What you will need: small cups of colorful beads.

- Give each child a cup of beads.
- Ask them to first sort the beads by color in a clean empty egg carton.
- Next, they will need to count how many beads they have of each color and write it down on the tally sheet provided in the worksheet appendix.
- While your guests are working on this, draw a graph on the wipe-off board.
- As a group, you are now ready to graph the totals.

Art: Butterflies

This activity celebrates the book *Fancy Nancy, Bonjour Butterfly* by Jane O'Connor.
What you will need: buttons, beads, feathers, glitter, glue, markers, crayons, colored pencils.

- Give each child a copy of the butterfly coloring sheet located in the worksheet appendix.
- Ask guests to make their butterfly fancy.

Technology

Log on to www.fancynancybooks.com to play Fancy Nancy games.
*Read more about the history of clothing at this Web site: http://www.history forkids.org/learn/clothing/

Party Snack

Dressed-Up Cookies

This activity celebrates the book *Fancy Nancy, Splendiforous Christmas* by Jane O'Connor.
What you will need: a premade sugar cookie for each guest, plastic knives, frosting divided into single serving cups, lots of colorful sprinkles and cookie decors.

- Show your guests how to spread frosting on their cookie using a plastic knife.
- Then, encourage them to make the cookies fancy with lots of sprinkles and decors.

26

Readers and Authors: Making a Lasting Connection

It's one thing for a child to be able to read a book, but an extra dimension is added when a child can connect with the book's creators. How do we as teachers, librarians, and parents connect our children, not only with a book, but also with the author and/or illustrator of that book? This chapter is dedicated to the many ways we can successfully make those connections.

Author Studies

Choose an author that is popular with your class or introduce them to a new author that could become a favorite.

- Read as many books as you can find by this author to your class. This will give your group the chance to really learn the tone and style of a particular author's voice.
- Try to read the titles in the order in which they were published. This gives children the opportunity to see and hear how the author's work has changed and grown over time.
- Read biographies of this author. The *Tenth Book of Junior Authors and Illustrators* provides biographies of 188 key figures in children's and young adult literature. Single biographies have been written for numerous favorite authors and illustrators.
- Visit YouTube and search for their book trailers.
- Don't forget to visit author Web sites, blogs, Facebook, and Twitter pages. These sources give a good picture of the artist's life and creative process.

Author Visits

The best way to make the connection is to arrange for a book creator (author or illustrator) visit to your school or library. Children can learn how creators come up with story ideas, the publishing process, and the review and marketing process. Above all, children will see that this wonderful rock star that they look up to and admire is a real living, breathing, human being who probably struggled with expository writing and/or art class as a child, too. They will realize that this goal of becoming a published writer or illustrator is attainable with hard work and perseverance.

Where to Find Authors

- The Society of Children's Book Writers and Illustrators has a Web site: http://www.scbwi.org/. If you click on Regional Chapters, they have a long list of chapter Web sites organized in alphabetical order by state/region. Most of these web sites have a speaker's directory that includes information about each author/illustrator's publishing credits and types of workshops that they offer.
- Check speaker's lists at the Author's Guild Web site: http://www.authors guild.org/ and The Children's Book Council site: http://www.cbcbooks.org/.
- A few other Web sites that may be able to help you find the perfect creator for your particular school or library are http://www.visitingauthors.com and http://www.authorsillustrators.com.
- Attend local reading council conferences, book fairs, and literary events in which authors and illustrators will be presenting. This gives you an opportunity to audition possible visitors. You can listen to their presentations, take note of their personality and style, and decide if this particular creator would be a good fit for your group.

Virtual Visits

Nothing will compare to a live author visit, but for schools with limited budgets, virtual visits can be a viable option. If you have a computer with a Web cam, you can do this. Visit Skype an Author Network: http://skypeanauthor.wetpaint.com/ to find a list of authors who do this type of visit. Learn the kinds of presentations they offer and how much they charge.

Funding School Visits

Costs for author visits vary widely. On average, honorariums for visits range from $200 to $1,000 per day plus food, lodging, and transportation costs. The more established an author is, the more expensive the visit is likely to be. The following is a list of ways to help your school or library fund a visit.

Cutting Costs

- Apply for a grant to cover the visit. The Society of Children's Book Writer's and Illustrators offers grants through their Amber Brown Fund, a tribute fund set up in honor of the late great Paula Danziger. Visit this link for more information on how to apply http://www.scbwi.org/Pages.aspx/Amber -Brown-Grant. Also, check with your local art council. They often provide grant funding for visits, too.
- Request sponsorship for a visit from local businesses and service organizations. Draft a letter of request detailing the need and how this will benefit children, estimated cost, what you will need specifically from them, and what

your school is willing to provide in the partnership. You could also ask for something simple in person or via a phone call. One of my school visits last year included a lunch donated by a local sandwich shop. The teachers and I had a great lunch, the school did not have to pay for it, and the local sandwich shop enjoyed free publicity in the form of a thank you printed the next week in the local paper.

- Make a deal. Authors are often flexible. Ask them about daily rate discounts if you book them for more than one day. Partner with another local school. You would have the author for half a day, the other school would have the author for half a day, and both schools would share the costs.
- Present the idea to your PTO, and ask them if they would be willing to come up with a fundraiser to cover the costs.
- Think local. Book creators live everywhere. In Illinois alone, we have almost 1,000 author and illustrator members of SCBWI. If you book someone locally, you are going to save big on food, lodging, and transportation costs.
- Think new. Often new authors, with only one or two published books, are willing to do visits for much less money than their more established peers.

Successful Visits

Please do not pass go without reading "How to Ensure a Terrific Visit"—a tip sheet compiled by Toni Buzzeo and Jane Kurtz authors of the book *Terrific Connections with Authors, Illustrators and Storytellers:* http://www.tonibuzzeo.com/visitsts good.html.

In Closing

I highly recommend the gift of an author/illustrator visit to your students. Give them the opportunity to meet these rock stars up close and personal. Give them the opportunity to get a book autographed. Give them the opportunity to have an extremely positive, life-long lasting impression of books and their creators. Give them the opportunity to see that their dream can also become a reality!

Appendix A

Party Invitation Templates

COME TO A

WILD BOOK RAMBLE

PLACE:_____

DATE:_____

TIME:_____

APPENDIX A
TEMPLATE 1

YOU'RE INVITED TO A
FAIRY TALE
FREE-FOR-ALL

PLACE:

DATE:

TIME:

APPENDIX A
TEMPLATE 2

ALL ABOARD THE
BOOK TRAIN

PLACE:_____

DATE:_____

TIME:_____

APPENDIX A
TEMPLATE 3

COME TO A BEAR BONANZA

PLACE:_____

DATE:_____

TIME:_____

APPENDIX A
TEMPLATE 4

COME
SEE

A Rainbow OF Reading FUN

PLACE:_____
DATE:_____
TIME:_____

APPENDIX A
TEMPLATE 5

From *Picture Book Parties!* by Kimberly M. Hutmacher.
Santa Barbara, CA: Libraries Unlimited. Copyright © 2011.

JOIN THE FRIEND FEST

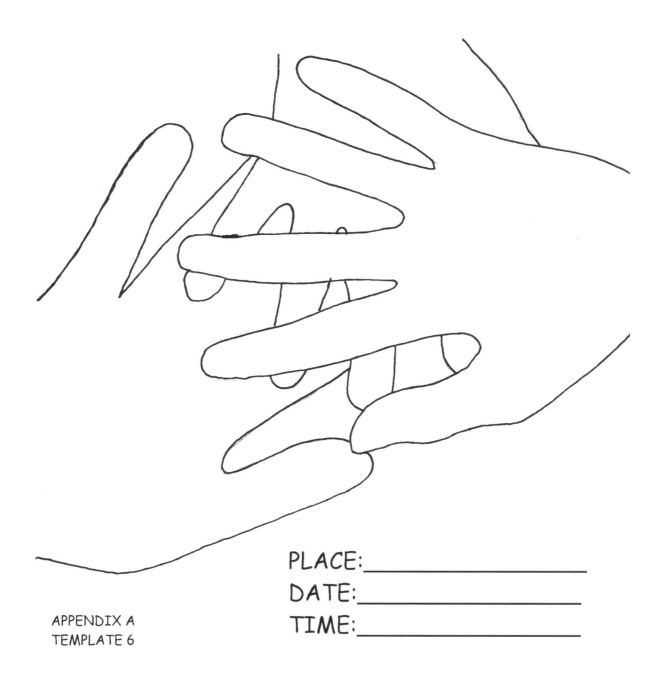

PLACE:_____
DATE:_____
TIME:_____

APPENDIX A
TEMPLATE 6

COME TO A
PIGEON PARTY

PLACE:_____

DATE:_____

TIME:_____

APPENDIX A
TEMPLATE 7

SOCKS
ROCK
PARTY

PLACE:_____

DATE:_____

TIME:_____

APPENDIX A   TEMPLATE 8

MOONLIGHT MADNESS PARTY

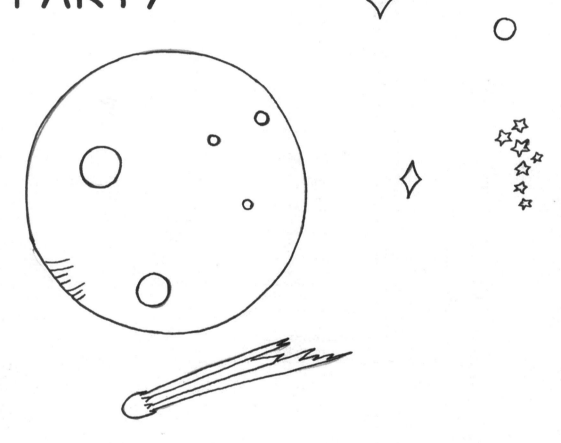

PLACE:_____

DATE:_____

TIME:_____

YOU'RE INVITED TO A BARNYARD BLOWOUT

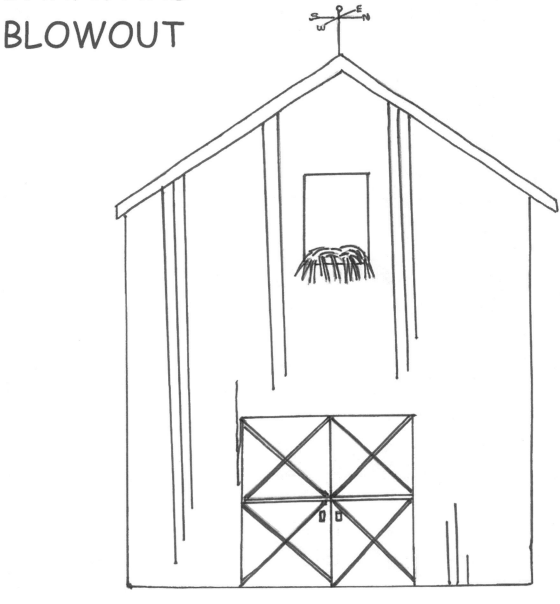

PLACE:_____

DATE:_____

TIME:_____

AWESOME
AUTUMN
PARTY

PLACE:_____

DATE:_____

TIME:_____

APPENDIX A TEMPLATE 11

COME TO A WINTER
WHIRLIGIG

DATE:_____

PLACE:_____

TIME:_____

APPPENDIX A
TEMPLATE 12

SPRING UP A GOOD STORY TODAY

PLACE:_____

DATE:_____

TIME:_____

APPENDIX A
TEMPLATE 13

SUMMER JUBILEE
PARTY

PLACE:_____

DATE:_____

TIME:_____

APPENDIX A
TEMPLATE 14

From *Picture Book Parties!* by Kimberly M. Hutmacher.
Santa Barbara, CA: Libraries Unlimited. Copyright © 2011.

COME TO A
GARDEN GALA

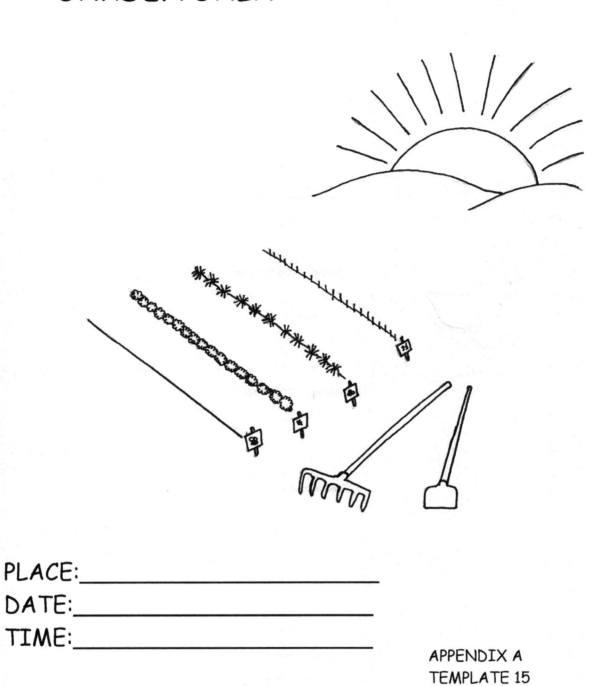

PLACE:_____

DATE:_____

TIME:_____

APPENDIX A
TEMPLATE 15

PLEASE ATTEND A
BACK TO SCHOOL BLAST

PLACE:_____

DATE:_____

TIME:_____

APPENDIX A
TEMPLATE 16

YOU'RE INVITED TO A
PIRATE PARTY

PLACE:_____

DATE:_____

TIME:_____

APPENDIX A
TEMPLATE 17

YOU'RE INVITED TO A
BIRTHDAY EXTRAVAGANZA

PLACE:_____

DATE:_____

TIME:_____

APPENDIX A
TEMPLATE 18

COME TO A
FAMILY FUN NIGHT

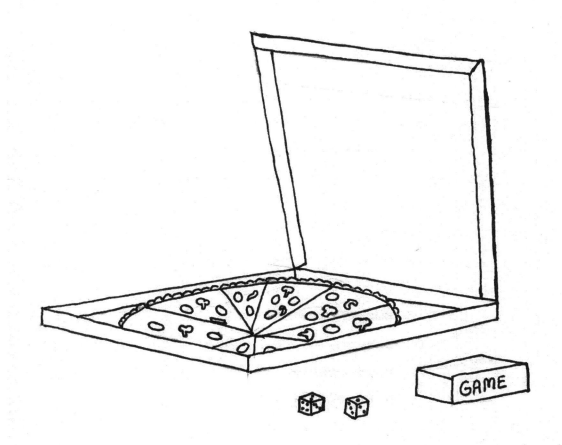

PLACE:_____

DATE:_____

TIME:_____

APPENDIX A
TEMPLATE 19

JUMP INTO A
RAIN RUMPUS

PLACE:_____

DATE:_____

TIME;_____

APPENDIX A
TEMPLATE 20

COME TO A
BIG TOP BASH

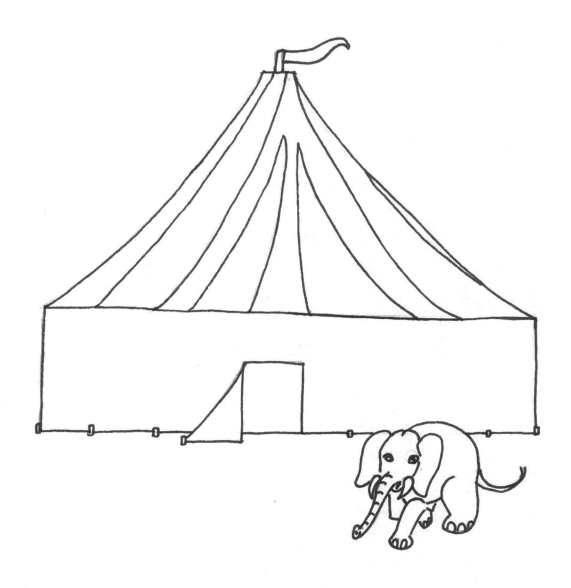

PLACE:_____

DATE:_____

TIME:_____

TEMPLATE A
APPENDIX 21

COME TO A
TOY SHOW AND TELL

PLACE:_____

DATE:_____

TIME:_____

APPENDIX A
TEMPLATE 22

COME JOIN THE
FISHING FUN

PLACE:_____

DATE:_____

TIME:_____

APPENDIX A
TEMPLATE 23

EVERYONE IS
BUGGIN' OUT

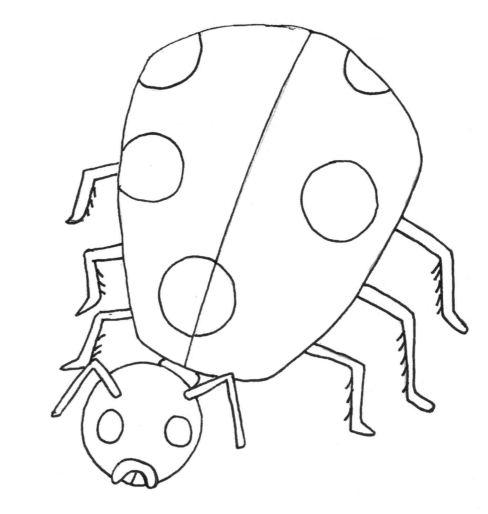

PLACE:_____

DATE:_____

TIME:_____

APPENDIX A
TEMPLATE 24

YOU'RE INVITED TO A
DRESS UP DAY

PLACE:_____

DATE:_____

TIME:_____

Appendix B

Center Activity and Game Templates

IF YOU WERE A FAIRY TALE CHARACTER . . .

WHAT KIND OF CHARACTER WOULD YOU BE?

_____

WHAT WOULD YOU LOOK LIKE?

_____

_____

_____

WHERE WOULD YOU LIVE?

_____

_____

WOULD YOU HAVE A JOB? IF SO, WHAT WOULD IT BE? IF NOT, HOW DO YOU
SPEND YOUR TIME?

_____

_____

_____

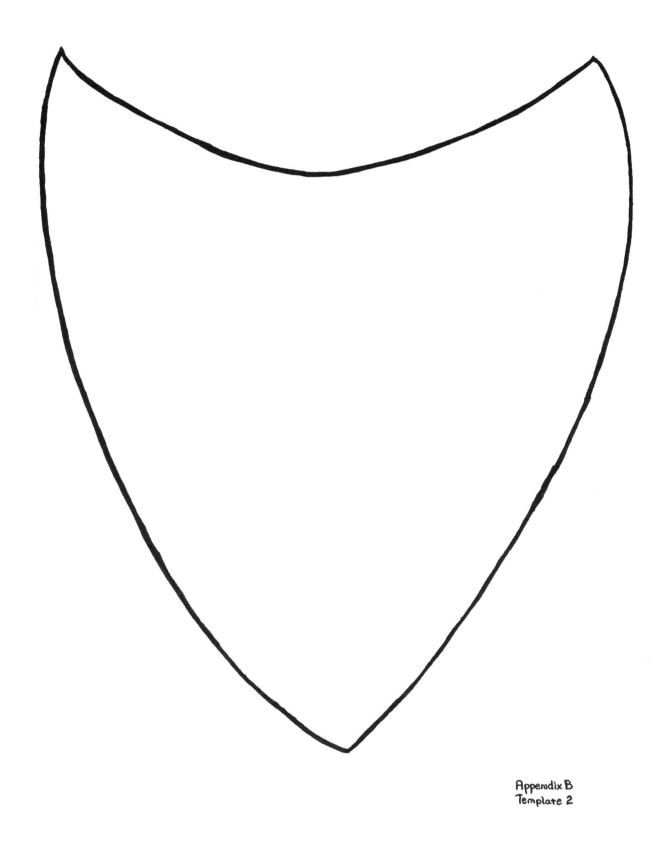

Appendix B
Template 2

APPENDIX B
TEMPLATE 4

APPENDIX B
TEMPLATE 5

Picture Book Bibliography

Ackerman, Karen. *Song and Dance Man*. New York: Knopf Books for Young Readers, 2003.

Auch, Mary Jane. *The Princess and the Pizza*. New York: Holiday House Inc., 2003.

Banks, Kate. *Mama's Coming Home*. New York: Farrar, Straus and Giroux Inc., 2003.

Barrett, Judi. *Benjamin's 365 Birthdays*. New York: Atheneum Books for Young Readers, 1992.

Barrett, Judi. *Cloudy With a Chance of Meatballs*. New York: Atheneum Books for Young Readers, 1978.

Bogacki, Tomek. *My First Garden*. New York: Farrar, Straus, and Giroux Inc., 2000.

Brett, Jan. *The Mitten* (20th Anniversary Edition). New York: Putnam, 2009.

Briggs, Raymond. *The Snowman*. New York: Random House Books for Young Readers, 1999.

Brown, Margaret Wise. *Goodnight Moon*. New York: HarperCollins Children's Books, 2005.

Brown, Margaret Wise. *Two Little Trains*. New York: HarperCollins Children's Books, 2003.

Bunting, Eve. *Pumpkin Fair*. New York: Sandpiper, 2001.

Carle, Eric. *A House for Hermit Crab* (World of Eric Carle). New York: Simon and Schuster Books for Young Readers, 2009.

Carle, Eric. *Papa, Please Get the Moon for Me*. New York: Simon, 1991.

Carle, Eric. *The Tiny Seed* (World of Eric Carle). New York: Little Simon, 2009.

Carle, Eric. *The Very Busy Spider*. New York: Philomel Books, 1989.

Carle, Eric. *The Very Hungry Caterpillar*. New York: Philomel Books, 1994.

Carle, Eric. *The Very Lonely Firefly*. New York: Philomel Books, 1995.

Carle, Eric. *The Very Quiet Cricket*. New York: Philomel Books, 1990.

Carlestrom, Nancy White. *Happy Birthday, Jesse Bear*. New York: Aladdin, 2000.

Clements, Andrew. *BIG AL*. New York: Atheneum Books for Young Readers, 1997.

Clements, Andrew. *Circus Family Dog*. New York: Sandpiper, 2008.

Clifton, Lucille. *The Boy Who Didn't Believe in Spring*. New York: Puffin Books, 1992.

Cooney, Barbara. *Miss Rumphius*. New York: Puffin Books, 1985.

Corey, Shana. *Milly and the Macy's Parade*. New York: Scholastic, 2006.

Cox, Judy. *Rabbit Pirates: A Tale of the Spinach Main*. New York: Scholastic, 2000.

Crelin, Bob. *Faces of the Moon*. Massachusetts: Charlesbridge Publishing, 2009.

Crews, Donald. *Freight Train*. New York: Scholastic, 1989.

Crews, Donald. *Night at the Fair*. New York: Greenwillow Books, 1998.

Crews, Nina. *One Hot Summer Day*. New York: Greenwillow Books, 1995.

Crimi, Carolyn. *Don't Need Friends*. New York: Dragonfly Books, 2001.

Cronin, Doreen. *Click, Clack, Moo: Cows That Type*. New York: Simon and Schuster Books for Young Readers, 2000.

Curlee, Lynn. *Trains*. New York: Atheneum Books for Young Readers, 2009.

Donalson, Julia. *The Gruffalo's Child*. New York: Puffin Books, 2007.

Earle, Sylvia. *Sea Critters*. Washington, DC: National Geographic Children's Books, 2000.

Egielski, Richard. *Slim and Jim*. New York: HarperCollins Children's Books, 2002.

Ehlert, Lois. *Growing Vegetable Soup*. New York: Sandpiper, 1991.

Ehlert, Lois. *Red Leaf, Yellow Leaf*. New York: Harcourt Children's Books, 1991.

Ehlert, Lois. *Snowballs*. New York: Sandpiper, 1999.

Ehrlich, H. M. *Louie's Goose*. New York: Sandpiper, 2002.

Emberley, Ed. *Go Away, Big Green Monster*. New York: Little, Brown and Company, 1992.

Fleming, Candace. *Muncha! Muncha! Muncha!* New York: Simon and Schuster/Atheneum, 2002.

Flora, James. *The Fabulous Firework Family*. New York: Margaret K. McElderry Books, 1994.

Fox, Mem. *Tough Boris*. New York: Sandpiper, 1998.

Freeman, Don. *Bearymore*. New York: Puffin Books, 1979.

Freeman, Don. *Corduroy* (40th Anniversary Edition). New York: Viking Children's Books, 2008.

Gibbons, Gail. *The Milk Makers*. New York: Aladdin, 1987.

Gibbons, Gail. *Pirates: Robbers of the High Seas*. New York: Little, Brown Young Readers, 1999.

Gill, Sherry. *Alaska's Three Bears*. Washington: Sasquatch Books, 2002.

Gottfried, Maya. *Last Night I Dreamed a Circus*. New York: Knopf Books for Young Readers, 2003.

Hatkoff, Isabella and Craig, Hatkoff. *Owen and Mzee: The True Story of a Remarkable Friendship*. New York: Scholastic Press, 2006.

Hausherr, Rosemarie. *Celebrating Families*. New York: Scholastic, 1997.

Henkes, Kevin. *Julius: The Baby of the World*. New York: Greenwillow Books, 1995.

Henkes, Kevin. *Kitten's First Full Moon*. New York: Greenwillow Books, 2004.

Hesse, Karen. *Come On, Rain!* New York: Scholastic Press, 1999.

Hines, Anna Grossnickle. *Daddy Makes the Best Spaghetti*. New York: Sandpiper, 1989.

Howe, James. *The Day the Teacher Went Bananas*. New York: Puffin Books, 1992.

Hughes, Shirley. *Dogger*. United Kingdom: Red Fox, 2008.

Hutchins, Pat. *It's My Birthday*. New York: Greenwillow Books, 1999.

Jackson, Alison. *There Was an Old Lady Who Swallowed a Pie*. New York: Puffin Books, 2002.

Jenkins, Steve. *Down, Down, Down*. Massachusetts: Houghton Mifflin Books for Children, 2009.

Johnson, Crockett. *Harold and the Purple Crayon* (50th Anniversary Edition). New York: Harper-Collins Children's Books, 1998.

Johnson, Neil. *Big Top Circus*. New York: Dial Books for Young Readers, 1995.

Keats, Ezra Jack. *The Snowy Day*. New York: Viking Children's Books, 1962.

Kennedy, Jimmy. *The Teddy Bear's Picnic*. New York: Aladdin, 2000.

Kindersley, Anabel and Barnabas, Kindersley. *Celebrations: Festivals, Carnivals, and Feast Days from around the World*. New York: DK Children, 1997.

Kinerk, Robert. *Timothy Cox Will Not Change His Socks*. New York: Simon and Schuster/Paula Wiseman, 2005.

Lasky, Kathryn. *Show and Tell Bunnies*. Massachusetts: Candlewick Press, 2001.

Latta, Sara L. *What Happens in Spring?* New Jersey: Enslow Elementary, 2006.

Latta, Sara L. *What Happens in Summer?* New Jersey: Enslow Elementary, 2006.

Lawlor, Laurie. *Where Will This Shoes Take You?: A Walk Through the History of Footwear*. New York: Walker and Company, 1996.

Leonni, Leo. *A Color of His Own*. New York: Knopf Books for Young Readers, 2006.

Lester, Helen. *Hooway for Wodney Wat*. New York: Sandpiper, 2002.

Lewis, Rose. *I Love You Like Crazy Cakes*. New York: Little, Brown Books for Young Readers, 2000.

Lobel, Arnold. *Frog and Toad Are Friends*. New York: HarperCollins Children's Books, 1970.

McClintock, Barbara. *Dahlia*. New York: Farrar, Straus and Giroux Inc., 2002.

McCloskey, Robert. *Blueberries for Sal*. New York: Viking Press, 1962.

McKissack, Patricia C. *A Million Fish . . . More or Less*. New York: Dragonfly Books, 1996.

McNamara, Margaret. *The Whistle on the Train*. New York: Hyperion Books for Children, 2008.

McNaughton, Colin. *Captain Abdul's Little Treasure* (with CD). Massachusetts: Candlewick Press, 2006.

McPhail, David. *The Puddle*. New York: Farrar, Straus and Giroux Inc., 2000.

McPhail, David. *The Teddy Bear*. New York: Henry Holt and Company, 2005.

Maguire, Jack. *Hopscotch, Hot Potato, and Ha Ha Ha*. Canada: Fireside, 1990.

Markle, Sandra. *A Rainy Day*. New York: Scholastic, 2002.

Markmann, Erika. *Grow It!* New York: Random House Books for Young Readers, 1991.

Martin, Jacqueline Briggs. *Snowflake Bentley*. New York: Sandpiper, 2009.

Martin Jr., Bill. *Brown Bear, Brown Bear, What Do You See?* (40th Anniversary Edition). New York: Henry Holt and Company, 2008.

Minarik, Else Holmelund. *It's Spring!* New York: Greenwillow Books, 1989.

Morton, Christine. *Picnic Farm*. New York: Holiday House Inc., 1998.

Munsch, Robert. *We Share Everything*. New York: Cartwheel Books, 2002.

O'Connor, Jane. *Fancy Nancy*. New York: HarperCollins Children's Books, 2005.

O'Connor, Jane. *Fancy Nancy and the Posh Puppy*. New York: HarperCollins Children's Books, 2007.

O'Connor, Jane. *Fancy Nancy, Bonjour Butterfly*. New York: HarperCollins Children's Books, 2008.

O'Connor, Jane. *Fancy Nancy, Splendiforous Christmas*. New York: HarperCollins Children's Books, 2009.

O'Malley, Kevin. *Once Upon a Cool Motorcycle Dude*. New York: Walker Books for Young Readers, 2005.

Penn, Audrey. *The Kissing Hand*. Indiana: Tanglewood Press, 2006.

Perritano, John. *Bugs on Your Body: Nature's Creepiest Creatures Live on You*. New York: Gareth Stevens Publishing, 2009.

Pfeffer, Wendy. *We Gather Together*. New York: Dutton Children's Books, 2006.

Pfister, Marcus. *The Rainbow Fish*. New York: Scholastic, Inc., 2000.

Ray, Mary Lyn. *Red Rubber Boot Day*. New York: Sandpiper, 2005.

Rohman, Eric. *My Friend Rabbit*. New York: Square Fish, 2007.

Rose, Deborah Lee. *Birthday Zoo*. Illinois: Albert Whitman & Company, 2002.

Rosen, Michael. *We're Going on a Bear Hunt* (Anniversary Edition). New York: Margaret K. McElderry Books, 2009.

Rosenberg, Liz. *Monster Mama*. New York: Putnam, 1997.

Schlein, Miriam. *Pigeons*. New York: Crowell, 1989.

Scieszka, Jon. *The Frog Prince Continued*. New York: Puffin Books, 1994.

Scieszka, Jon. The *Stinky Cheese Man and Other Fairly Stupid Tales*. New York: Viking Children's Books, 1992.

Sendak, Maurice. *Where the Wild Things Are*. New York: HarperCollins Children's Books, 1988.

Shannon, David. *Duck on a Bike*. New York: Houghton Mifflin Harcourt, 2006.

Shea, Bob. *New Socks*. New York: Little, Brown Books for Young Readers, 2007.

Dr. Seuss. *The Cat in the Hat*. New York: Random House Books for Young Readers, 1957.

Dr. Seuss. *Fox in Socks*. New York: Random House Inc., 1965.

Dr. Seuss. *My Many Colored Days*. New York: Knopf Books for Young Readers, 1996.

Steele, Philip. *Toys and Games*. New York: Franklin Watts, 2000.

Sullivan, Charles. *Circus*. New York: Rizzoli International Publications, 1992.

Tolhurst, Marilyn. *Somebody and the Three Blairs*. New York: Scholastic, 1994.

Tucker, Kathy. *Do Pirates Take Baths?* Illinois: Albert Whitman & Company, 1997.

Van Allsberg, Chris. *Jumanji*. New York: Houghton Mifflin Books for Children, 1981.

Van Allsberg, Chris. *The Polar Express*. New York: Houghton Mifflin Books for Children, 1985.

Van Laan, Nancy. *Little Fish, Lost*. New York: Aladdin, 2001.

Warne, L. Rowland. *Eye Witness:* Costume. New York: DK Children, 2000.

Westray, Kathleen. *A Color Sampler*. New York: Houghton Mifflin, 1993.

Willems, Mo. *Don't Let the Pigeon Drive the Bus*. New York: Hyperion Books for Children, 2003.

Willems, Mo. *Don't Let the Pigeon Stay Up Late*. New York: Hyperion Books for Children, 2006.

Willems, Mo. *The Pigeon Finds a Hot Dog*. New York: Hyperion Books for Children, 2004.

Willems, Mo. *The Pigeon Wants a Puppy*. New York: Hyperion Books for Children, 2008.

Windsor, Merrill. *Baby Farm Animals*. Washington, DC: National Geographic Society, 1985.

Yolen, Jane. *Owl Moon*. New York: Philomel Books, 1987.

Ziefert, Harriet. *10 Little Sock Monkeys*. New York: Sterling Publishing Company, 2005.

Index

About the Author

KIMBERLY M. HUTMACHER is the former poetry editor for *Wee Ones Magazine*, a book reviewer and the author of 14 books and over 60 pieces of poetry, fiction, and nonfiction for the magazine market. She teaches creative writing classes for both adults and children. Kimberly says, "I enjoy sharing my passion for writing as much as I enjoy writing itself." Kimberly provides inspirational and educational workshops for children and adults. You can learn more about Kimberly, her books and her workshop offerings by visiting her Web site at http://www.kimberlyhutmacher.com/bio.html. You can also read reviews of her favorite nonfiction picture books for children at the Wild About Nature blog http://wildaboutnaturewriters.blogspot.com/.